Julian Chitta

SCIENTIFIC
SUPERSTITIONS

SCIENTIFIC SUPERSTITIONS
Julian Chitta

C O N T E N T S

INTRODUCTION
A discussion on research methodology and how the
scientific superstitions are born

With the general erosion of the education, world-wide, many scientific concepts are forgotten, obscured or hidden, in the quest to promote certain points of view, which will generate the necessary funds from patrons. Most of the time those underwriters of scientific research are governments with definite agendas.

Tragically, the academia and the press jump on the line towed through "official theories" and any dissenting positions are eliminated without discourse.

The most elementary approach to scientific research is perverted to an ideological stance reducing the chances for any hypothesis to be proven or tested. That's how many questionable theories are based solely on hypothesis, without facts derived from scientific observation, or from experimentation.

The most notorious examples that come to mind are the "global warming" (later changed to "climate change"), the "population explosion" and tectonic disasters that are just about to happen.

Traditionally, a hypothesis is verified through experimentation and observation. If the result of observations and experiments do not confirm it, the hypothesis is discharged and a new one is selected. If the results, however, are coincidental with the elements of the hypothesis, and they can be duplicated through experiments, the hypothesis is deemed to be valid. This way of advancing scientific research has been consecrated even since antiquity.

A hypothesis has a limited life span. It cannot be absolutely and definitely proven, but rather it becomes an accepted theory, since at one time or another, it survived the barrage of scrutiny through "scientific" testing, and has been accepted as "true". If the scope of the observation and experimentation is widened enough, the original hypothesis will lose some of its first luster. A new hypothesis challenges an old one. And since the technology advanced since the old hypothesis was last visited, the acuity of this process of observation allows for an expanded variation in conclusions. The old hypothesis is discharged and the new one is deemed to predict better the elements of its object. If the new hypothesis can satisfy the predictability factors, it will survive.

Just think about the number of "electrical theories" circulated during the last two centuries:

- the electric charges are of a metaphysical nature;
- they flow from positive to negative;
- they flow from negative to positive;
- they don't "flow', they just move electrons at orbital level;
- it is an exchange of "holes' and electrons at atomic level;
- it is a form of chemical energy that alters and reconstructs atoms;
- it is just like a "domino" effect, etc.

Every single theory captivated the scientists for few decades, until the next one was better explained, and so on. This aspect of "scientific thinking" was present in every field of human activity, resulting in rapid changes and re-evaluations of the research philosophy and the methods used..

There was no time, in recent history, when the keystone discoveries were not ridiculed by the "scientific establishment", yet, today, they are considered basic elements in our Type II civilization (When the humans were able to leave the planet)

This paradox of scientific research and discoveries is responsible for the fact that the most important technological advances occurred outside the academia and totally independent of the circles of consecrated scientists.

Just think of the automobile, oscilloscope, airplane, computer, etc.

The perverting of scientific work starts with the very idea of defining, in advance, all the concepts and terms to be underlined philosophically.

When most of the variables are inventoried, and an algorithm has been selected, the essential research becomes conditioned by the parameters of the sponsor, be it any educational institution, industrial concern or a government subdivision.

The scientific factors, the accuracy of experiments and the type of data collected are all, of secondary importance to the sponsor's main objective.

That objective carries a tremendous ideological load that the scientist cannot jettison. It is the entity that foots the bills for the research, having the ultimate say in everything, especially in the area of results and conclusions.

And at this point the reasoning gets infested by superstition. The most virulent, camouflaged, pretexts that defy logic, can be simply defined as "scientific superstitions". It permeates equally all fields of scientific research. Its existence can only be justified by the chase for research grants, salaries, tenure, and greed.

This aspect of scientific work is equivalent to the sins found in the executive world of captains of industry and their remuneration schemes, however, the scientist becomes a virtually destitute as soon as a separation from his or her work occurs.

How many people can employ a highly trained PhD in multiple disciplines, with a very highly specialized experience for unique applications yet to be born?

The Soviet government kept its scientist in high esteem, paid them well, but did not allow them the individual freedom needed to nurture creativity. Everything was according to a plan devised by party officials. With rare exceptions, their "inspiration" to create technological marvels came from America.

USA, on the other hand, used a similar approach, especially within the confines of the system labeled as the "military-industrial complex" by Dwight D. Eisenhower. The radicalization of America and Western Europe, with a marked move to the left, has determined the proliferation of scores of pseudo-scientific pronouncements that illustrate quite well this bubble of scientific superstition.

If a Hollywood actor, who never took a class in physics or chemistry, comes all over the media proclaiming that the sky is falling, due to flatulence caused by cows, and the immense mass of ignorant consumers "buy" it wholeheartedly, the effect of a mass hysteria is very easy to engineer, especially, if the governments want to eliminate the small farmers and ranchers, in favor of the corporate mega operations. (It is easier to work with one single entity, with plenty of money, than with thousands of small ones that are on the verge of bankruptcy. Small operators are notoriously inferior to corporate agro-business enterprises in the area of electoral contributions.)

Nevertheless, the scientific superstitions are here to stay, and the erosion of the education our children get, is a guarantee for their survival, but do not think, for a second, that America is unique in this respect. So is the European Union, Russia, China and many Muslim countries, most notably Iran.

The science is an excellent propaganda medium and it is less risky to use, as compared to print or electronic media. The rumors surrounding scientific research are so valuable in this respect that many regimes cannot survive without them.

How is it that scientific superstitions find such a fertile ground in "advanced" societies, where the educational level of the population is deemed superior? Simply by "superficial penetration". It creates something similar to a "Faraday Cage" that will not permit any logic to penetrate it, to get to its core inside.

It is relatively simple to debunk the majority of scientific superstitions, which are purveyed at every public level. The problems consist, however, in the personality clash between Hollywood role-models and anonymous college professors who rarely get any exposure. Who would be trusted and who would be listened to? The glamorous one!

Thus that is an irrefutable proof that the sky is falling. I heard it on TV!

The perversion of scientific research, tailored to fit certain ideological lines of thought, becomes deeper as the economic picture darkens. Less available funds, chased by a lot more "scientists", causes the elimination of those with fragile political ties. The scope of the research, its depth and perceived benefits, if finished, do not account hardly for anything, if they don't fit the agenda of the sponsor.

It has been reported that in the 20s, Nicola Tesla proposed a system of free energy, for everybody, and got through advanced research, partially subsidized by J. P. Morgan, who did not want to hear about "such an aberration". There had to be a way to collect money from such a convenience. People become lazy if they get free stuff! And the research funds for Tesla were all cut off. We will never know what we are missing.

Such a relationship, between sponsors and research scientists, moves along the ebbs and flows of political tides.

The word "superstition" comes from the Latin "superstitio" which means to "stand over", or to "place above", most of the time in disbelief or amazement, as a certain notion with religious substrate. As a matter of belief, soon the term "superstition" was used in conjunction with practices not sanctioned by the Church.

The scientific superstitions are born, in majority, from a process of thinking that places the accent of research on correlation and not on causation. Thus coincidences may offer a preponderant conclusion that is not always supported by data. And that's the way a superstition creeps in, rendering the entire research questionable.

There is a practice, well established since the XVII century that can be defined as "net casting" or "data dredging", which, in itself may be a viable tool that can skew the results in a desired direction. That's the way the famous "theory" of instantaneous creation was established. It simply stated that decaying matter, flesh and skin of mammals, is prone to this phenomenon. The apparition of maggots was thus justified. All the data pointed to this "theory". And the examples were overwhelming, all provided by consecrated scientists of the day. We aren't any different today.

The "Post hoc", (Latin for "after this") analysis by which data is scanned for certain relationships, coincidental to the experiment and observation objectives, has nothing to do with the actual scientific method. It creates "statistics" that can be "sustained". That approach eliminates incentives for honest research, institutionalizing "pure" statistics, which, most of the time were "fabricated".

The good side of this approach consists in a progressive multiplication of the hypothesis elements, at times causing the researchers to "stumble' on discoveries. That's the point of convergence of science and superstition. (Scientific superstition, that is.)

Nevertheless, superstitions run circles around academia, before the scientific truth makes its first steps. And that is the straw that breaks the camel's back.

I'm not a scientist, academician, or a researcher. In my career I had to take for granted all the scientific "dictates", as they applied to my field of work in electrical and electronic applications. I used simple, down to earth, reasoning, based on elementary physics and mathematics, as my training allowed it. I used the results of giants in those fields, together with modern technologies that became available just recently, to find ways to solve practical problems. That's when the questionable aspects of modern science became evident. Working on analysis of "Mean Time to Failure" for aircraft parts, was no statistical picnic, and you had to sort and eliminate insignificant elements of many of the "sanctioned" statistical methods. A variance can be negligible when you sort pebbles, but it can mean matters of life and death when it comes to airplane integrity, especially when it is based on a hypothesis of component feasibility to perform.

That's why I started to question most of the research methods imposed by various regulatory authorities. The minimum statistical basis is just not enough for certain things. A practical person shall go beyond that limitation. In engineering and design that fact becomes quite evident, however, the needs of cost containment alter this approach. It is OK if you deal with a video game or an article of clothing, but a totally different thing in the field of medical equipment and pharmaceuticals.

Why do you think so many medications are rejected off the bat, or removed from the market after few years of damages to unsuspecting users?

That's because the research process was short-circuited and the blank spaces were filled in with scientific superstitions.

Who are the regulators (plain bureaucrats) or the consumer (plain ignoramuses) to question the calculations, the algorithm, the method or the statistical interpretation of the data collected by seasoned specialists? Since it was created by such "specialists", with absolutely pristine credentials as the "innovators" of the industry .

The market forces, which have the bad habit of promoting the best products at the lowest price, can reduce anybody's profits, through fierce competition. That's when the regulators would earn their salaries, by deciding how to promote their darlings of the industry, through the funding of research. (Hitler did that amazingly well.) No one is immune to this highly charged political bias, regardless the industry. With all frankness, the regulators are the major purveyors of scientific superstitions, followed by the academia and its members, who are under tremendous pressure to publish and to register patents.

I don't think that the prevalent affirmations, about the inefficiency of the consecrated institutionalized scientific superstitions, are off the mark. That field seems to have evolved into a distinct industry, all by itself, with all elements of a well-structured industrial operation, with R&D, manufacturing, sales and service. The odd aspect however, is the willing participation of the news media in supporting and advertising all such aspects.

In the following chapters of this book I propose to examine some the most blatant cases of scientific superstition perpetrated upon an unsuspecting public. My approach is simple, requiring a minimum of scientific knowledge, of the type one gets as a freshman in college, and it will point to the major fallacies that require a strong faith just to survive, since the facts negate every single hypothesis that starts the whole mess.

"If your ideas don't match the facts, change the facts". Mark Twain said it best, without suspecting that it would characterize so accurately the scientific work, some one hundred years later.

Please note that there are many exceptions to this shocking practice, and my hat goes off to those dedicated industrious scientific workers. They all deserve our thanks.

Emblematic of the situation created by the convergence between a elitist society based on technology, and the oppressed members of the "working class", starved for even the most basic commodities, is the defunct Soviet model.

Politicos, technocrats, military and the academia, cultivated the need to justify the scientific culture ideologically, and most every country in the world copied that model, reminiscent of the Nazi practices of the 1930's. The symbiotic relation between science and ideology created alternating ebbs and flows of period of intense development for new technologies and industries. Recent history points to the examples of Japan, Germany, Korea, and China.. Is that a positive or a negative circumstance?

In spite of the multifaceted progress of a new industrial revolution based on the processing of natural resource, a significant segment of the modern society remains in a position of subservience to the governmental social assistance programs.

Very few "scientists" raise the issue of life quality. Most of us can use better means of transportation, we use better food, have better homes, etc., yet our index of satisfaction with our stations in life continues to fall under the pressure of the day-to-day stress. Perhaps the most shocking paradox of the life on this planet, is offered by the fact that in spite of the ability to create sections of bionic humans, we are much less able to insure a healthy society.

In the drive to impose artificial concepts upon the most innovative representatives of the scientific society, the government's thrust is felt like a shock wave. It is a fact of life with strange consequences. The notion that an inventor or researcher could not be "qualified" to handle his or her brain child may looks ridiculous, yet it is a very common occurrence. A FBI agents come and confiscate personal papers because a lone wolf came upon a crucial discovery, outside the parameters allowed. Urban legend describe novel laser, radar, spectroscopy, d radio wave and biological applications which have been hijacked by the government's agents, because the inventor had no security clearances, yet he or she was the one to pioneer those new technologies. How can anyone qualify such acts other than theft of intellectual property?

The lone researcher, putting long hours in his own private laboratory, after longer hours worked for his employer, in totally unrelated fields, is victimized twice. Once by the system, and the second time by the innuendos and gag orders meant to create solid scientific superstitions surrounding us.

2. Quantum Mechanics and Parallel Universes

How mathematicians and physicists "bend" the semantics to obtain "effects" that justify their points of view.

Quantum mechanics, or quantum physics, is a branch of the science which tries to establish mathematically a uniform law for the relationship between matter and energy, based on a "wave function" that is found to be germane to absolutely everything. The quantum theories are, all founded on mathematical probability and do not require extraordinary means to work.

Most of the theories based on quantum principles seem to work extremely well at atomic level, where the interaction between protons, electrons and neutrons can be explained mathematically.

Max Plank (1858-1947), a German physicist, who is credited with much of the pioneering work in this field, has coined the term "quanta", representing a minute change in electron behavior, hence the name of the discipline.

It is a well-known fact that quantum mechanics can satisfy the most exigent conditions of research at atomic level, in a micro-dynamic state. It can explain well angular motion, angular momentum and orbital elements regarding electron movement along fixed or variable atomic orbits.

From that point on, the characteristics of "wave function", at atomic level can be evaluated through classical physics concepts, such as harmonic wave oscillation, resonance, peak values, etc.

The "old quantum theory" was adequate for establishing mathematical relations at micro-dynamic levels. The problems started to creep in when a lot of "innovative researchers" tried to expand the quantum physics concepts to macro-dynamic levels, into the realm of astronomic dimensions.

They observed that all matter follows a similar existential pattern. An atom has a nucleus; all planetary systems have a nucleus. Both have satellite elements orbiting them on determined trajectories with predictable variations. In both systems, be they micro or macro, the energetic balance is kept through matter, and both can be practically ascertained in most details.

When divorcing the confines of our own planetary system, in order to step into the galactic area, misusing the term "universe", the theoretical positions of most modern scientists cannot be sustained.

By examining the semantic essence of the word "universe", it is very easy to see that to "swallow" it by a single formula or a unique mathematical function would be a very tall order. Trying to come up with a bullet-proof, an all-encompassing formula, capable to "explain" everything, borders on arrogance. Albert Einstein (1879-1955), did try that, with his theory of relativity, to the extent that he systematized the knowledge accumulated by previous generations of scientists, in the same manner geniuses like Antoine Lavoisier (1743-1794), and Dmitri Mendeleev (1834-1907), established the laws of periodic variations in the table of elements. Some scientists consider that the jury is still out on Albert Einstein's theory.

Some of the earliest definitions of the word "universe" were absolute: "the totality of everything that exists". During the Renaissance the definition was expanded to include "all things physical or spiritual". During the 19th century, German philosophers went a step further, defining the universe as "the space which starts at the locus of the observer, and expands in absolutely every direction, to infinity." (They also defined two parallel lines as two lines that intersect at a point known as "infinity.")

From a modern point of view, the "universe" is universal, has no beginning and no end. This implies that no matter in which direction you travel, no matter for how many billions of years, even at the speed of light, you will always, remain within the universe, since it has no limits.

And this concept of "no limits", goes contrary to the basic tenets of quantum mechanics, which assigns origination points and ends point to anything, be it matter, energy or an interactions in time.

The very acceptance of the notion of "universe" precludes anything outside of it. Any galaxy, solar system, world or spatial subdivision is, therefore, a part of the universe.

Introducing the notion of "Parallel Universes", modern scientists create the false hypothesis that there is a possibility for the existence of "multiple universes". Logically, any such element would be just a part, a sub-set of the universe. If you can only have one item, how can you get it to have a parallel?

William James (1842-1910), a trained physician, educator and a theologian, advanced the idea of the "multi-verses" or parallel universes, as an illustration of divine perfection, yet he admitted that: "No human, today, can fully comprehend the marvel of universal creation."

In the earlier part of the 20th century, his ideas have been rediscovered by academia, and his thesis of parallel multi-verses, metaverses, kataverses, has been allowed to penetrate most all scientific fields, from cosmology and astronomy, to physics, psychology and religious philosophy.

Since none of these notions could withstand the most elementary scrutiny, to anyone's surprise, the scientists took religion to their defense. Anything not mathematically demonstrable was attributed to God. One of these direct results was the creation of a model simply defined as the "Hubble Sphere".

That is the totality of the space surrounding an observer, like a sphere, which causes the vanishing of all objects at a certain distance. That was not explained as a shortcoming of visual physiology, but as due to universe's expansion at the speed of light. In other words, we can't see certain distant objects, not because our poor vision, but because those objects are moving away from us, at the speed of light (186,282 miles a second, or 299,792 km per second) No one was ever able to prove or disprove this theory.

Certain celestial formations are the result of spatial movement, such as galaxies, solar or planetary systems, and can be very well documented with spectral measurements of reflected light, in Doppler mode.

The Doppler Effect consists in the tendency of the radiation to decrease in frequency, if the emission point moves away from the observer. That causes the visible portion of the spectrum, the light, to undergo a shift toward a lower frequency. (Red). No arguments here. But to deduct that there is a parallel universe that functions on different laws of physics, totally negating basic universal interactions of matter, energy in time, is, at best, a fallacy.

The confusion does not end here. Enter the specific notion of "Hubble Volume" (named after Edwin Hubble 1889-1953), and try to apply it out of its original context, as the "observable universe", and try to determine which one is the largest. Both the Hubble Volume and the observable volume are sub-sets of the universe, which is unique. Any notion of parallelism to itself is a non-sense, even though this theory comes with an elegant exit, by establishing the so-called Hubble Limit, which identifies the edge of the Hubble space.

All the corollary theories can work in this context, if you only will consider your space of observation as limited, and most importantly, very separate and distinct from the whole of the universe, as a subset.

The only legitimate use of a process of thinking based on "parallel universes" is in the domain of science fiction.

Too bad that very few scientists can detect such a pure distinction. In the Hubble theory the universe expands, yet in a different approach, that of Alexander Friedman (1888-1925) the hypothesis of a shrinking universe is presented as an element that causes the continuous expansion of the Hubble volume, but the Russian physicist could not benefit from modern spectrum analysis nor from exchanges with the American counterparts, thus creating the impression of unfinished essay. Thus one can view his work as based strictly on a false hypothesis.

It does not take a great deal of scientific training to deduct that if you accept the semantic notion of "universe", at its most common usage, you have to exclude the possibility of anything existing outside its domain.

And that includes parallel universes.

Mathematics can't prove a negative, even though some stubborn academics try hard to invalidate common sense and logic. They place the label "quantum" on anything that defies elementary understanding.

Recent scientific papers that advance the ideas of "Universe 1",and"Uni-verse 2", etc., accept an arrangement in a form similar to the strings of a musical instrument, thus subject to the laws of mechanical oscillations, vibration, harmonics and resonance, but do not offer much beyond an elegant approach to scientific suppositions.

Few of the most realistic researchers are asking for the substantial revisions for the currently accepted norms of research, trying to establish a common-sense vocabulary to elements yet to be discovered. Semantics will prove an undisputed connection between poetry and science. (For a wider popular acceptance some will even mix religion with it.)

Since an axiom or a postulate is a supposition, or a proposition that cannot be proven with the tools offered by the system used, then the current crop of theories, anchored in quantum assumptions, remain just that: some elegant exercises in original thinking. Is that science or superstition?

In my modest opinion the term "parallel universes" has to be replaced by "parallel subsets" of the universe. This way most of the quantum theories would be applicable to the immense astronomical scales, and the confusion could be reduced, but not totally eliminated .

The quantum mechanics is an excellent tool, just like a hammer is for a builder. But when the main tool you have is the hammer, then all your problems seem to look like nails. That's when hitting a nail on the head is much more important than where you place the nail, and the superstition creeps in, granting false credits to people who are rarely questioned.

The fashionable trend of divorcing scientific thinking, from the basic elements of classical mathematics. and physics, in terms of the relations, between matter, energy and time, scores high on the list of labels that start with the obscure qualifier of "original thinking" and end up with a false "theoretical validity", as an irrefutable theory.

That is scientific superstition at its best!

Luckily, fewer and fewer Americans have the educational background or the inclination to survey this field of quantum relations, since abstract or Suppositional thinking is highly discouraged by the academia.

3.The Tip of the Iceberg
The issue of climate change revisited, based on simple physics

Not long ago, in a Midwestern city, the high school seniors did their annual prank on the unsuspecting inhabitants, by distributing leaflets, all over the city, with the following content:

"Citizens, this is to inform you that the city's Utilities Department is pumping, day and night, **hydrogen oxide** into your homes, and you have no idea how this is being done. In minute quantities the hydrogen oxide is harmless. If you increase the quantity, it can cause severe diarrhea, while, if inhaled in excess, will produce death, through asphyxia. Every year, over 1,700 persons, in the USA alone, die because of excessive inhalation of hydrogen oxide. Are you next?"

That resulted in an unmanageable assault on the city hall, by angry residents, with the mayor unable to explain what the "hydrogen oxide" was.
"Hydrogen oxide" is plain water. The chemical identifier is derived from the water's composition, which consists of one oxygen atom and two, bonded, hydrogen atoms, as H-O-H, thus hydrogen oxide.
So much for what the public knows about water. Of course, if taken in excess may cause diarrhea, and if inhaled – like in the case of a drowning – it may cause death.
I selected this example to illustrate the general public's position when bombarded, ad nauseam, with various "theories", including those of global warming , recently renamed as "climate change".
The most spectacular effect of the so-called climate change, is fanned by media, as a "scientific warning" about the melting of world's ice deposits and the unprecedented rise in sea levels, which undoubtedly will flood entire coastal areas, all over the world.
I would term such a supposition simply a clear example of scientific superstition. I base this opinion on simple physical facts and geodesic data, readily available from various sources, both objective and subjective.
Allow me to examine a few factors that should have been entered into the "calculations". The melting of ice on Earth is a natural phenomenon, and, it is a major contributor to climate parameters.

The water occupies some 70% of our planets surface and ice is an allotropic form of water, or, in other words, it is just solidified water. The liquid is the most commonly known form, followed by its solid form, ice, and gas, like atmospheric water vapors. Nothing new, here, however the water is the most important climate-determining element. It affects the hydrosphere, atmosphere, geosphere, biosphere, plants and animals. Thus the water, at all levels is an important life and weather regulator.

The water has a very definite cycle, from evaporation to precipitation, to runoff. Snow, hail and ice formations are an integral part of this cycle. No one disagrees with this fact, yet many "scientific" theories and specialized interpretations flaunt the simplest logic. The total area of the globe, covered by ice, including the polar caps, represents some 3.5%

Freezing water expands 8.0% in volume.

A simple-minded conclusion would be that if the entire ice melts, the ocean levels would drop by some 9.0%. I said "simple-minded" because not all ice is in the oceans and not all the ice melts into water. Some 50% of the ice which is above the water, (or ground), does not melt. It sublimates. It is transformed directly from a solid state to a vapor state, and it dissipates into the atmosphere.

According to most recent geodesic data, the approximate amount of water evaporated over the oceans, is about 96 Tt (Trillion tons) per year. Some of it will precipitate over the water, while a smaller amount will be carried over land. The amount of water vapor in the air, over continental masses, is estimated at some 40 Tt per year. The total precipitation, over land, averages more than 25 Tt per year. The winds and solar activity, together with this water cycle determine the global climate.

The apocalyptic spectrum of ice melting, due to "severe" temperature increases, is, at best, an unfounded hypothesis. During the last 50 years the world's temperature increased by 0.68°C.

Geologically, the world has known temperature swings, of some 5°C up and down, over long periods of time, resulting in centuries of mini ice ages, or extremely hot periods. At one time, some 92,000 years ago, Sahara was a lush-vegetation tropical paradise, while some 900 years ago the polar ice cap reached today's Denmark. Greenland was named so, by the Vikings, due to its forests of pine trees. Today, that landmass is just an icy rock.

Increases in temperatures are started by increased solar activity. That causes ice to melt. Melting ice absorbs thermal energy, as an endothermic physical phenomenon, thus reducing the ambient temperature. Freezing water releases thermal energy. That aspect is extremely significant for the auto-control of the weather engine.

Collectively, all the ice in the world is known to form the cryosphere. That includes mountain ice and packed snow, sea ice, submerged, floating or anchored to shores, land ice and polar ice. Some estimates place the quantity of sea ice at 70 Tt while the land ice is approximately 170 Tt. Under most prevailing conditions of sun, wind, etc. only some 10% of ice melts while another 10% sublimates directly into the atmosphere. Even under such marginal conditions, the extra water drained into the oceans, may cause a 300 cm drop in sea levels. Under such an aspect no one accounts for the evaporation of sea water, "de minimis" another 15%.

Each ton of melting ice removes one kilo calorie of thermal energy per centigrade, from the atmosphere. (Can anyone estimate the effect of several trillion tons of ice melting?)

Several "competent" authors, published between 1980 and 1990. predicted that by the year 2000 the entire Florida Coast would be under three feet of salt water. They missed the mark!

Other "prestigious" books cite the frequency of hurricanes and many unusual weather patterns as proof of irreversible "climate change". The fact that there were no reliable weather recordings older than 150 years reduces the statistical basis of any such "studies", to the point of irrelevance.

The weather patterns are determined by the jet stream movement and position, forming cyclones and anticyclones in both hemispheres. The globe rotation causes Coriolis forces to affect the path of moving weather systems, including anticyclones originating on the west coast of Africa.

That's why an anti-cyclone has a tendency to curve to the right, in the Northern Hemisphere and in opposite direction below the equator. The same holds true for Pacific taifuns originated from the South American continent. Any weather system, be it high (cyclone) or low atmospheric pressure, (anti-cyclone), creates ideal weather distribution only if it keeps moving. Certain conditions, such as jet stream inertia, can cause them to linger on stationary coordinates for relatively long periods of time. That causes either drought or floods, depending on geography. The melting of the ice (or not) has nothing to do with such systemic irregularities.

One interesting aspect of polar ice melting was observed years after the famous eruption of the Krakatoa volcano, (1883). The years of solar radiation obstruction, by the volcanic ash dispersed into the atmosphere, dropped the average temperatures by some 5° C causing years "without a summer". In spite of that direct effect of cooling, the polar ice was melting at an accelerated pace.

The observations made by the scientists of that period explained the phenomenon as being caused by "embedded volcanic ash" on the surface of ice masses. Darker in color, it absorbed considerable more solar heat energy triggering an unprecedented ice melting, while the rest of the world was shivering under a darkened sun. Roald Amundsen, (1872-1927), the famous polar explorer, observed, and described this unusual circumstance, during his 1910 and 1912 Antarctic explorations. He found volcanic ash in ice, at depths of 2-3 feet, some 25 years after the Krakatoa eruption. The ice at that level had a distinct, "shiny" aspect associated with melting. The weather patterns over most of the world, at that time, were "normal".

An entire series of books, printed after 2000, try to explain that the "observed climate changes have already affected a variety of physical and biological systems", with the firm conclusion that the human activity, (read "existence"), is responsible for all the unusual weather patterns, causing an alarming decline in the amount of "environmental ice", including polar caps.

One specific "study", which originated in 1999, in England, tries to set the problems of climate change in proper perspective, claiming that the temperatures are rising, as evidenced by a smaller number of icebergs off the Iceland's coasts, concluding that this is "just the tip of the iceberg." (Any salt-water iceberg would display, above the waterline, only some 15% of its mass.)

The assumption that a severe climate change is due to human activity, known as the thesis of anthropogenic cause of "global warming", has a lot of supporters and opponents, none being able to come with irrefutable data. One of the flaws in related scientific fields has to do with an economic bias, since all the participants receive grants to prove or disprove a point. Even if your measurements are correct, if they do not coincide with your sponsor's agenda, they will remain buried. Another flaw consists in the limited data available concerning historical weather observations. You have to use a statistical collection of data, at best, over a span of only 150 years, to project it into the future. You have no access to real data concerning millions of years of climate phenomena on this Earth. The only authority "capable" to validate your research is the sponsor who pays for your work. How objective that can be?

As the saying goes, if you only see the tip of the iceberg, how can you guesstimate what is under the water, if you do not have the right tools to go to see for yourself?

85% of the iceberg mass can take many forms, can extend in many unexpected directions, and can take on several colors.

Predicting the trends in weather changes just by studying the tip of the iceberg, is like judging a book by its cover, so don't be surprised if I'll tell you that all the systems on this planet are in a process of constant change: hydrosphere, atmosphere, cryosphere, geosphere and biosphere.

All of a sudden the tip of the iceberg looks, very much, like a shiny diamond: very expensive.

Several scandals around the scientific circles studying "climate change", in UK and USA, made the news once or twice, and were ignored afterwards, while Hollywood types crowded the tabloids and the TV screens with their "scientific conclusions" that we, all, are going to drown in the waves of water coming from melting polar ice caps.

Some Arctic and Antarctic expeditions documented the collapse and the fragmentation of certain sections of polar ice fields.

When new layers of ice pile up on the top of an old ice mass the weight of those additional millions of tons will place a tremendous pressure on the bottom layer, causing melting. That undermines the basic physical integrity of the entire ice mass, causing fissures, breaks and erosion. That leads, ultimately, to the disintegration of the lower part of the ice mass. It is a normal, continuous cycle which never stops, even if the high local diabatic winds will maintain temperatures well below the -60 degrees C mark.

You can rest assured that a lot of water molecules in the water you drink, originated in such a place. The transportation mechanism for that was considered compliments of the Jetstream. But that is only partially true.

When sea salt water freezes, the caloric exchange, that takes place at approximately -3.0° C, changes the salinity distribution, in fact removing the salt out of the mass of freezing sea water. That would change the salt water density, close to that of the fresh water. This phenomenon known as "brine rejection" , causes the formation of a layer of water, colder, with higher salinity just below the newly formed ice. The denser and colder salt water sinks, migrating toward the bottom. The dynamic of the resulting vertical movement, which induces horizontal currents, is poorly understood today. The only certitude is offered by the measurements which indicate without any doubt that the heavier, more concentrated sea water, on the bottom of the oceans, is pushed away from the polar regions, generating definite areas of separation between strata of water, in terms of temperature and salinity, along the thermocline lines. A drastic change in deep polar currents may have unfortunate consequences upon the climate of certain latitudes. That alternates accumulations of sea ice from high volume to minimal volume, shaping the thermal loads on the surface of large masses of water.

Most of the land-based glacial ice goes through similar cyclical phases of collapsing, rebounding and sliding on an incline. The weight of ice causes its bottom to melt, providing a natural lubricant for its migration.

Getting alarmed about such a natural phenomenon and proclaiming that the Apocalypse is here, is equivalent to stopping at the sight of a black cat. (No sense in continuing, since your bad luck has been "confirmed".)

The Iceland's Academy of Science, has a much more practical take on this ice melting scenario. Dr. Thor Markeson, of the University of Iceland, in a paper published in 2005, stated unequivocally that:

"… There is a marked difference between some scientists who makes one scientific field trip to the world's ice areas, and those of us who live and work here. Some populations have observed icebergs for generations, and learned to interpret changes in their behavior correctly, unlike the visitors who pontificate over the simplest aspects of ice mass movements, spewing ridiculous theories that cannot be sustained logically".

The fact that Iceland is a unique geological laboratory, as a small land mass, surrounded by cold waters, offering thermal pictures that go from the sub-freezing marks, to the high temperatures of molten volcanic lava, gives the scientists the opportunity to place in proper perspective all data that can Be collected now.

That makes a huge difference in the methodology used in a laboratory set up, in an academic institution, vis-à-vis the hands-on approach a student of meteorology can use in Iceland or anywhere else.

Most dedicated scientists can see that the statistical basis they can have access to, is quite limited, thus abstaining to formulate outlandish or unfounded theories. Since they avoid to make any kind of earth-shaking declarations, they do not benefit of unlimited funding, for their research, bucking the axiom of the golden rule, according to which, the one with the gold, makes the rules, and sets the agenda.

Most pronouncements, about the alarming climate change, have been issued in the comfort of a cozy office, and not in a cold field laboratory, thus offering anyone, another clear example of a scientific superstition.

One of the most revealing points of view about meteorology, are those of the farmers who advise you, to be patient, because sooner or later the local weather will change. It always does.

4. Missing Link   4.

Human evolution theories rejected by the academia

The scientific consensus, regarding human evolution, has been, for over one century, that the erect humanoid appeared first in East Africa, and due to specific geographic characteristics, evolved from there to the form known as the "homo erectus", which culminated with "homo sapiens".

This theory was widely accepted and forms the main core of most all anthropological theories of human evolution. The very few fossil remains do have a gap that spans millions of years, thus the notion of "missing link" was adopted to account for such inconsistencies.

Most of the explanations regarding this lack of plausible data would fall within the realm of "scientific superstitions". They are entrenched so deeply into the academic mind set that any hypothesis not coincidental in every respect with such "theories" is deemed suspect, and their authors are marginalized.

The German pathologist (and "amateur" anthropologist), Dr. Max Westenhoeffer, (1899-1959), working for the Nazi government , advanced, in 1942, a hypothesis that the human race evolved from primates that lived near or in the water, concluding that the researchers are looking in the wrong places to find the "missing link".

His studies came under the label of the "aquatic ape theory", which, in the beginning earned him the scorn of his colleagues, who were charged to document scientifically the Arian race's superiority. Later, after the end of the war, the marine biologist, Allister Hardy (1896-1985), and the geologist Christopher Harrison (1900-1986), both from England, provided some morphologic and physiological evidence that the original humanoids were better suited for an aquatic life than for the arboreal environment all the scientists connect with apes and early humanoids.

The academia and the scientific community rejected vehemently this hypothesis, on account of lack of proper "scientific" credentials for all who subscribed to "this ridiculous idea". Who ever heard of an aquatic ape?

To make the things worse, Elaine Morgan, (1920-2012), a Welsh writer, subscribed to this point of view and has written several books on this subject popularizing the aquatic ape theory, to the dismay of the scientific establishment. In 1997, John H. Langdon, published several articles, and a peer reviewed paper, criticizing the supporters of the aquatic ape theory, as "amateurish" because it was based entirely on a deductive process on one single, isolated "causal mechanism", that falls outside the "accepted research norms".

The supporters of the aquatic ape theory pointed to a set of features in the humans that are not common to apes, suggesting that rather the water environment played the most crucial role in the natural selection process.

Critics argue that such claims will support only a fraction of the such argumentation, since there are no fossil records.

The paleoanthropologists cannot reject any of the points presented in support of the aquatic ape theory, however, they select to ignore them as not coinciding with the prevailing lines of reasoning in the academia:

Erection and bipedalism. A definite change in posture, by maintaining an erect body, walking vertically on two legs, is a condition of importance when searching for food in fresh or salt water, much more so than what it would be needed to climb trees for fruits or bird eggs. Thus the human foot, different from that of an ape, seems to be perfectly adapted for swimming. The ape foot resembles the hand, thus better suited for climbing trees.

Lungs and larynx. The human chest is exceptionally suited to house lungs that can inhale and "hold" the breath for relatively long periods of time. The human larynx is located in the throat, and not in the nasal cavity, like the apes have it. That permits vocalization. It was observed, by biologists, that all the animals that are capable to "hold air", vocalize for communications. That is a common characteristic in birds and in aquatic mammals. All the dolphins, the wales, walruses and the seals have that ability. It was assumed that the humans developed articulated speech that way, since the sound modulations are much better transmitted under water. From articulated words to abstract reasoning, during over one million years, or so, can be more than sufficient to reach human characteristics.

Hairlessness. The human bodies vary greatly in the amount of hair and its distribution. Some biologists have observed that the human hair grows following the same line water would flow off the body. That it is an indication that the aquatic ape did not spend all the time in water, (Aquatic mammals have thick hair, to provide thermal insulation.) In contrast, the apes sport thick hair, which in tropical climates helps insulate the body against tropical heat. To keep cool, the human body perspires, and lack of thick hair helps the evaporation. Apes don't perspire. Their thick hair simply shields them from the sun.

Brain development. Proponents advanced the idea that the human encephalization process was only possible due to a diet rich in fatty acids found in fish. A land-based alimentation cannot provide those basic nutrients for brain development. Most of the human fossils which were dated to periods of 4 - 5 million years ago show a cranial capacity similar to that of the gorillas. Obviously, we should look for different fossils.

The American anthropologist, John D. Hawks, from the University of Wisconsin in attacking the aquatic ape theory, explains that even though an evolutionary process determined by the circumstances imposed by life in the proximity of water may be plausible, some theoretical considerations cannot be accepted:

"This is why professional anthropologists reject this theory, even if they have not examined all the arguments and have not fully thought through the logic."

That is another example of rejecting a hypothesis because of its origin, and not because its essence. That's how scientific superstitions are born.

Some of the more sensible arguments against the aquatic ape theory come from some scientists that accept the fact that early humanoids may have foraged under water and may have lived near flooded areas, but if one would connect that to evolutionary adaptation, that would have occurred much later than initially proposed. That may have happened during the Pleistocene period, (2 to 5 million years ago), and not during the Pliocene period. (5 to 10 million years ago)

What's 2 or 10 million years in the Earth's geological history of over 4.5 billion years? A small dot on a map!

If the human race was able to transit from a Type I civilization status, (a primitive society), to a Type II civilization, (technological, capable to leave the planet), in only 3-5,000 years, then it would be conceivable to accept that, possibly, some branches of the human tree developed into the exceptionally adapted subspecies. Where are the vestiges of such humanoid groups? Possibly buried, miles deep, under the tectonic plates which did undergo millions of years of overlapping . Most likely that's where all the aquatic ape skeletons are, together with all the remnants of their dwellings and artifacts.

At one time it was an absolute "truth" that the Earth was only some seven thousand years old, according to obtuse Bible interpretations. To voice any opinion contrary to that, even if supported by facts, was a punishable offense. Scientific superstitions are awfully intolerant.

Would it be possible that a few centuries from now, the science world would have a different view on the missing link?

The subject of aquatic apes came to unexpected prominence when a TV crew filmed some marine mammals using walrus bones as tools, in the act of subduing large Pacific fish. That demonstrated reasoning, social group cooperation and communication. When some Alaska natives were shown that footage, they told the producer that they have seen "mermaids" before. As unbelievable at it seems, several populations on the Pacific Rim feature the notion of mermaids as an important folkloric element. Primitive people in India, Australia and Africa, all have the mermaid image in their ancestral folkloric tales. Is that the direction in which all the anthropological research should be driven to find the fossils of the aquatic ape?

When in 1974, in Ethiopia, a humanoid fossil was discovered by Dr. Donald Johnson, dated to over 3 million years, it was assumed that one of the most important links in the gap of human evolution was finally bridged. That fossil of an Australopithocus afarensis, nicknamed Lucy, was found in a layer of volcanic ash, much younger than the estimated geological age of the surrounding area, raised serious doubts as to the validity of some thesis advanced by the anthropologists. Among the first to voice criticism upon the conclusions of Dr. Donald Johnson's team, was Dr. Londa Schiebinger, who found inconsistencies in the assessment of Lucy's gender and skeletal characteristics. Accordingly, Lucy was not a 100% erect humanoid, thus being more likely an extinct species of ape. Thus it appears that the full "Homo erectus" could not have been older than one million years. The point on which no one disputes the time the "Homo sapiens" appeared, in Africa, is approximately the 200,000 years mark. One of the most difficult elements to ascertain is the causal relationship with the local geography, far away from any significant body of water, fact which, possibly did cause a massive migrations to Europe and Asia. At that time the social groups of Homo sapiens seem to have been centered on a well-structured family and tribe life, yet the connection between them is at best sketchy.

The chain of evolutionary human fossils does not allow, at this time, the insertion of an aquatic ape, even though there is a gap between 500,000 and 200,000 years, on the geological clock, with some 5% differences.

5. Scientific Superstitions in Schools

How the "education scientists" destroy our youth

Education "experts" in America are trying to impose upon the tax-paying public, several biased concepts that fall in the category of scientific superstitions, Most of that nonsense is justified through "altruistic" ideas that those that do not perform in the field of learning, may get quite damaged psychologically, with lost self-esteem. To avoid that, the grading system, in many schools, is being eliminated, as "technologically obsolete".

The same champions of "scientific pedagogy" eliminate certain high skills that tax young brains too much. Both the extremely low skills and the extremely high skills are headed for the chopping block.

The surprising explanation, that we have plenty of specialists who can be tapped for help, in real life, does not hold any water.

Some educational scientists consider learning to write long-hand, with Latin characters a loss of time. Dr. Barbara Brower of the Los Angeles, CA school district, stated few years ago that:

"Drilling young students to write long-hand, in the age of computer printers, is a non-sense. If anyone would need to read historical documents written in long hand, they will have to learn that skill in the college. That is a gross waste of time and resources, just like forcing algebra and calculus upon high school students. That places minorities at a disadvantage, and we cannot allow that form of discrimination."

Some states jumped immediately on that bandwagon legislating that some simple tasks, like learning to write with cursive letters and using penmanship, are considered "primitive" thus needing to be eliminated from the curriculum. So do a lot of "high skill" disciplines, mostly in mathematic fields.

The Latin expression "aurea mediocritas", did never intend to mean that mediocrity is golden, rather that a "middle approach" is golden.

Eliminating both low and high skills, from the educational process, would be equivalent to reversing society's progress. The net result of such an obtuse approach would be a dumber society.

Contrast that with the educational systems of India, China or Japan, where high school students can outperform American college graduates.

Leading states in this "crusade" to dumb America down are, in order California, Illinois, Michigan and New York. Someone said that an army marches on its stomach. The victory is determined by food calories. By a simple extension, one can affirm that a society, a civilization, or a nation survives through its brains. Failing to properly develop the brains of our school children, through structured quality education, sets us on a fast path to self-destruction, no matter what kind of money the education bureaucrats get. Spending over $ 20,000 per year, per student, in our public education, guarantees the survival of the opinion that the process is more important than the result. The education has become an industry and its captains are only interested in making money and not in educating their charges.

Eliminating top-skill and low-skill chores makes their life easier.

Let's take a look at calculus, as an "unnecessary high skill".

Early scientists like Sir Isaac Newton. (1643-1727) and Leonhard Euler, (1707-1783), in trying to decipher the basic laws of the universe, found out that the mathematics of the day could not offer the proper tools to ascertain any of the characteristics of bodies in motion, be they celestial or simply falling apples. So the study of motion had to invent and to use a new mathematical branch, the calculus. The word is derived from the Latin "calculus", representing a stone pebble used in counting sacks of wheat, or heads of livestock to be turned over as taxes.

The notions of variables, trajectory and speed, together with their corollary aspects of acceleration and kinetic energy, was too much for the mathematics of the day that barely could handle two variables at a time.

Calculus was invented in the seventeenth and eighteenth century, simply to provide the tool to ascertain and explain simple mechanical phenomena, which presented the aspects of constant change in space and time. It enabled scientists, for the first time, to define slopes of lines and curves, to calculate velocity and acceleration.

The most important advantage brought by the use of calculus, was the ability to predict, exactly, future positions of objects in motion, with an amazing degree of accuracy.

As a complement of mathematical analysis, calculus can solve today, extremely complex problems in various scientific fields, from engineering to astronomy.

The mastery of calculus is a necessity for the modern technocrat, and no substitute could offer valid solutions, even though "educational experts", all over the world, would tell you differently. First, learning to handle calculus, as a discipline, is different from mastering core concepts in the fields of arithmetic, algebra or geometry. In those subjects you learn the mechanics of handling expressions with some variables. Calculus uses some of the elements from arithmetic, algebra and geometry, but it introduces, from its very beginning, new concepts and computational techniques.

The rewards of learning calculus, consist in increased options for those who seek professional careers, aside from a significant degree of personal satisfaction. Calculus is a necessity, for a Type II civilization, such as our technological society, capable to leave the planet, but our esteemed education "experts" miss that boat.

Calculus establishes that the derivative of every constant function is the "zero function". Education "experts", however, insist on the zero-sum.

Eliminating the teaching of certain subjects in our schools, on account that they pose an undue stress on young minds, as an overly high-level skill, does benefit no one, except the administrators who can deal now with less problems.

Going to the lower extreme, that of simple-skill subjects, the school administrations, in several states, have removed penmanship and long-hand writing out of their curricula. The move, recommended by "specialists", will create generations of adults unable to write a simple card or letter. The lame justification, that "the age of computers and printers makes that particular skill obsolete", means practically, the creation of a large underclass of young intellectual invalids.

In a scientific sense, the education should be the process of knowledge transfer from one generation to the next. In reality, however, the education is everything one retains after forgetting most of the things learned in school. And that notion of "school" includes everything: primary, secondary or post-secondary education.

Reducing the amount of knowledge, available to the current young generation, does not improve anything, except, perhaps, the expense line in the school budget. Justifying that with "scientific means" is a superstition that is being proliferated to the detriment of all the future generations.

The Americans' right to basic education, guaranteed by virtually every single state constitution, is subject to local review only, in terms of curricular content and structure. And that is of lower importance for most electorates, just behind football and finances. (Read school taxes).

Some argue that any educational system in the world is designed to create some special classes of citizens, such as bureaucrats, soldiers, and workers. Historically that was the case with many other countries, (France, Germany, Japan, Russia, China, India, etc.), while here, in the USA, under the umbrella of an education geared to individual needs, the objective was to create taxpayers, and obviously, a lesser-educated taxpayer is a much better taxpayer.

That is a virulent superstition from the field of "scientific" education. The North American Consortium for Education, LLC, a think tank that does analyze educational trends and advises school boards on curriculum matters, opposes the elimination of school subjects based on biased opinions from the part of the education bureaucrats. Surprisingly enough, the labor unions, the National Education Association, (NEA), and many other similar groups , go along with this aberration of reducing the 'teaching load".

Many researchers in the field of education came to the consensus that a school should develop the skills necessary for logical reasoning, scientific inquiry, in order to establish the basis for the future agents of change. The main purpose of a school is to teach the students how to think independently.

But since most of the schools are tied to a system of "measurements" for "results", through all sorts of standardized tests, the accent is not placed upon the knowledge transfer, but on the ability to pass those tests. In other words, the schools teach how to pass standardized tests. And that is a waste of efforts, money and time. That's why many high school graduates cannot read or write, nor can give change to one dollar if the "machine" is down.

The public education is one of the fields in which the creeping in of scientific superstitions does the most damage to the society.

A former head of the NEA, described, in 1974, without using the term "scientific superstitions" in education, some aspects that came to fruition much earlier than it was anticipated:

"Operating a school, without physical and intellectual discipline will nurture the formation of a next generation of adults, with no respect for law, without morals, or work ethic, accustomed to operate in a gang atmosphere, with all the corollaries that go with that: drugs, violence and illegitimate children. Of course, the rest of the society will have to pay for that dearly."

The damages caused by applying scientific superstitions in the field of education, are severe and long lasting. It will take the sacrifice of several generations, just to recuperate from that social impact.

That's exactly what happened in Mao's China, during the infamous "Cultural Revolution", when the school curricula were reduced only to the reading and memorizing the text of the little "Red Book". College professors and students were sent to distant rural communities, for "re-education" through manual labor. It took China two generations to correct some of the damages done by the process of elevating superstition above the science.

Let's hope that America will not copy the Chinese model, here.

6. Time Revisited
Ridiculous "new" theories about time

In May 2012, two scientists from the University of Barcelona, in Spain, Dr. Alberto Yzaguire and Dr. Traian Voica, published a paper in the Spanish scientific literature, "Time Revisited", advancing the theory that the time will come to a total standstill, in about 3.5 billion years.

Two other scientists, Dr. Emilio Berlanga and Dr. Fritz Egon, from the University of Salamanca, also in Spain, analyzed that paper and came with some proposals to correct the original computations.

Their approach suggested a different set of calculations that would yield a correction of some 1.6 billion years that would place that event much earlier.

The world of scientists was perplexed, since the approach was logical and the calculations made sense. Scientific magazines carried reviews of the "Time Revisited" paper, on all continents. Publications like Daily Mail, in UK, Oggi, in Italy, Stern, in Germany, and even China Daily did explain this new "theory" in a simple, popular style, for their readers. There were some voices, mostly in USA and Japan, which discounted this "theory" as pure "speculation".

Ozuki Fukuyama, signed an article in the Tokyo's prestigious Nihon Keizai, that the Spanish scientists just "signed the birth certificate of a new scientific superstition". That article was carried by several other publications in Japan, like the Kobe Shinbun and Kyoto Shinbun.

A journalist for China Daily wrote, tongue in chick, that "with certain mathematical dexterity one can prove almost anything, simply because very few people can handle overly abstract notions."

Dr. Jose Senovilla, from the Basque University of Bilbao, Spain, takes the side of his colleagues from Barcelona and Salamanca, writing for the New Scientist magazine. He states that at the moment the time stops, our solar system would already be vanished, since the expansion of the universe is equivalent to an explosion, of which we are utterly unaware.

Support for this new theory came from the most unexpected places.

Dr. Raymond Higgins, a cosmologist with the Cambridge University in England, advances the view that "since the time appeared at the moment the Big Bang was produced, it is only natural that at some certain point it will disappear. It is a reciprocal action natural to all phenomena."

Then, what is time?

Time could only be defined as a continuous indefinite progress of all existence, irreversible, in progressive flow originated in the past. Time is an element that allows mental comparisons of sequential variations. All the events one observes take place on a constant line of action started in the past, continued through the present and headed into the future, but this temporal element is much harder to understand than a simple reference to what any clock measures: the passing of time.

Many ancient civilizations, including Hebrews and Hindus did not have in their language a present tense. The reason was that if you talk about an action, it gets to be consumed "by the past", before you know about it. Everything happened in the past or it will happen in the future. Nothing can happen "right now".

In modern science time is one of the seven fundamental units of measurement codified under the International System of Measurement, or the ISM. Time is essential in determining certain parameters for all common elements of observation, such as changes in speed and acceleration.

Historically, the philosophy toiled with the task of defining the time. Subsequently, several theories were developed, each of which being deemed extremely useful at the time of its adoption by the scientific community. Two basic approaches were used, over the years. One was the linear nature of time, to which Sir Isaac Newton, (1642-1727), subscribed fully. That theory replaced the "circular theory" of time, used by the ancients. Greeks, Romans, Persians and Egyptians, who conceived the time like a universal wheel, on which everything occurred cyclically. That satisfied most everything, from the celestial body movements, to the seasonal weather changes.

The concept of "time travel" is possible in both directions with the circular model just mentioned.

Another point of view, that of time's absolute independence from anything material, was justified by the human brain's ability to "invent" abstract notions, like numbers and time. German philosophers like Gottfried Leibniz, (1716-1646), and Immanuel Kant, (1724-1804) subscribed to this point of view postulating that the time is not a physical entity, thus it cannot be measured accurately, nor it can be travelled.

The measurement of time, however, became a pressing necessity during the age of early sea navigators.

Ray Cummings, (1887-2008), an early writer of science fiction, wrote in 1923 that the notion of time, "...is simply what keeps everything from happening all at once."

This approach in understanding time was adopted by many scientist of stature, like John Archibald Wheeler, (1911-2008) from the University of Texas at Austin. The Canadian scientist, C.J. Overton, did not add lot to the Cummings definition that "...time is what the clock shows."

The English word "clock" is probably derived from the Saxon or Gaelic words "glocke", or "clocke", which are derivatives of the old Latin "clocca", meaning bell, Churches, monasteries and ships at sea marked the passing of the time with bells.

The German scientist Dr. Albert Richter, in an article in the Nature magazine, referring to the "Time Revisited" paper, stated that the authors do recognize and accept the fact that: "... the time is basically an existential element, justified only through the experience of the observer. Thus, if the observer dies, there is nothing to observe. The time dies with the observer!"

Out of all these discussions about the characteristics of time, as a unit of measurement with definite physical or mathematical nuances, some M I T researchers revisited an ancient quasi-cyclical concept of time inspired by Archimedes of Syracuse, (287-212 BC), who invented the Archimedes' spiral and, during the Middle Ages, some astronomers converted it to a tool for practical time measurements.

Applying the Archimedes' spiral to time measurements can satisfy both the linear and the circular time theories. Starting at the point of origin, the time line expands toward infinity at increasingly higher peripheral speed in constant angular motion.

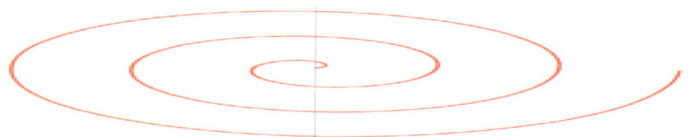

Archimedes' spiral satisfies both linear and circular time ideas. If you can devise increments to define days, months, years, centuries and millennia, you could handle well geologic or astronomical elements of time. However, if you need to go the other way, into the difficult realm of smaller time subdivisions like milliseconds, microseconds or nanoseconds, you only can rely on special instruments, that have to convert such abstract notions into light signals, or into the bleeps of some cathode ray tubes. Was the time invented by the human brain? Will the time disappear, if the electricity is cut off?

7. The Science of Economics
How the leftists try to destroy America through false theories

As a social science that analyzes the production, the distribution and the consumption of goods and services, the economics field is subject to most political influences and it is infested by many superstitions of very dubious origins perhaps, tied to ideological pressure, more than any other discipline.

The words economics and economy are derived from Greek, and mean, literally, "to manage a household". ("Oikos" means house, or home, while "nomos" means rule", thus the word "oikonomos" was adopted as "economy", meaning the science of administering a household. Of course, over the last centuries its semantic was extended to signify today's meaning.

The basic methods of economic research are centered on mathematics and on statistical analysis.

The Scottish philosopher John Adams (1723-1790) was one of the first scientific economists, who pioneered the research methods used today. His main work was "An Inquiry into the Nature and the Causes of the Wealth of Nations". (Abbreviated as "The Wealth of Nations")

Today there are several terms that did not capture the attention of the pioneers of economic research, such as microeconomics (the study of small economic units, firms, corporations or administrative divisions) or that of macroeconomics (the study of economy at state, continental or global levels). That's simply because those terms have been "invented" only during the second half of the 20th century.

John Adams was one of the first scientists to discover and to point to the basic elements of capitalism, the new economic force born after the fall of the feudal system, during the birth of the industrial revolution.

He correctly identified the importance of markets, and the process of accumulating wealth through profits generated in commerce and industry.

Today the economists divide the world economies into two basic groups, in part based on John Adams' astute observations, as market economies, (The capitalist models based on free enterprise), and the non-market economies (The fascist, socialist, communist models where the government plans everything, dictating who can produce what, and who can buy)

The first scientific superstition to be adopted, in this respect, was the assumption that the US economy is a market economy, when in fact it has most of the characteristics germane to non-market economies: the US government regulates strictly everything, from hiring, to production and to sales. The government becomes a major partner in every single economic act, just like it was in the now-defunct Soviet Union, where everything was based on a governmental decree. The US government is practicing the same concepts of planned economic activities in most every sector, after starting, in the late 1940s with agriculture and mining. Many farmers were paid not to produce certain crops, etc. (Any subsidized industry becomes subservient to the one who dishes out the cash.)

The capitalist realities of the period, presented flaws, which John Adams explained elegantly as "contractions" and "expansions" of trade, a fact which underlined why some nations are wealthier than others.

Karl Marx (1818-1883) was familiar with John Adams work, and in his book, "The Capital", ("Das Kapital"), published in 1863, he asserts that the advancement of the human race was due to a dialectic class struggle of continuous nature, between have's and have-not's, between capital and labor and between land-owner and land-worker, etc.

Most of Marx's observations were valid for the feudal society that just preceded the industrial revolution, yet he applied his findings to a totally different society, where the fuel of economic progress was the technology.

Marx drew his conclusions from the experience of his contemporaries, most of them German revolutionaries, socialists or anarchists, signing as an author, together with Friedrich Engels (1820-1896).

The economic model of the day, advanced by Karl Marx, was the erroneous scheme, based on the notion that the capital is the lethal force that will always keep the worker in bondage to his job.

He invented an elaborate scheme to demonstrate his points, based on a process in which the "input" was fixed or variable capital, the "processing" segment consisted in the complete dehumanization of the worker, (the force of production), while the "output" was the profit for the owner of the means of production.

The notion of market and free exchange of values, between producers and consumers escaped him. He could not comprehend the existence or the needs of a middle class.

His "capitalistic economic model" was simply a superstition based on contorted relations between the elements Karl Marx considered important.

His justification in "analyzing" the economic realities of that period was to facilitate the creation of a "proletarian dictatorship".

Karl Marx was never able to ascertain the elements of the economic models of capitalism, which in its simplest form resembles a pyramid. The apex is occupied by the "Research and Development" function, the next layers representing the manufacturing, sales and service phases. It should be noted that the first two layers, R&D, and manufacturing operations, are both capital intensive. The sales part of the model is the only income producing operation. The last layer, the "service" operation, supports the sales efforts. The pyramid has three sides. Two sides deal with capitalization and the investment of retained profits. This model fits all types of organizations and every field of economic activity, from banks and insurance companies to coal mines and airlines.

Which element is the most important in the economic equation? A true solution would be offered by the word "all".

Capitalization, personnel and process, are absolutely vital elements, yet the profitt can be elusive outside a synchronized action that exercises all the necessary components, based on a very simple relation.

Personnel + Capital + Process = Profit

The personnel represents the entrepreneurs, the managers and the technicians who handle the appropriate technology.

The capital consists of certain assets, loans, retained profits, and accounts receivable.

The process is the actual connection between the proper input elements, such as raw materials, subassemblies, etc. and the output of the process, the finished product.

The relationship between all the costs involved in keeping the personnel the capital and the process, at an adequate level, versus the money obtained through the sale of finished products, is one of the magic words of business: profit.

That is the engine that powers the modern society, making all other things possible. By all means, it is not a dirty word, as most all the leftist claim, and it keeps a lot of minds busy to invent a new, better mouse trap.

That's what keeps the markets open, for all participants who want to do business.

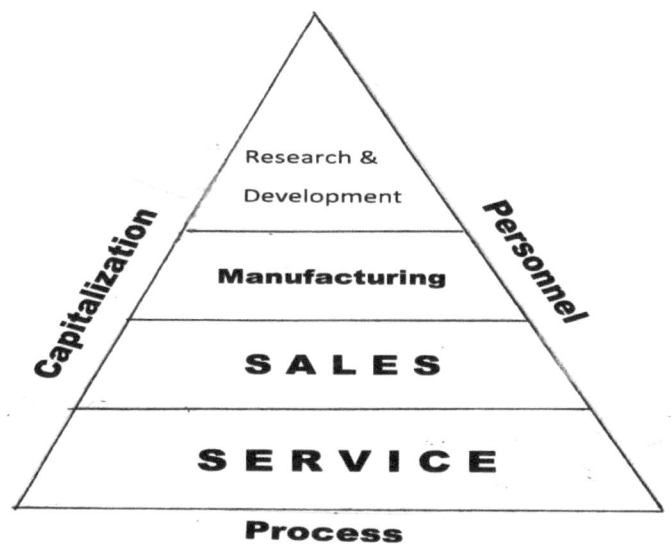

The universal modern economic model

Please note that in the diagram of the modern economic model, each one of the four sectors represents, proportionately the capital outlays, as needed for the entire operation. Thus the Research and Development, (R & D), together with the Manufacturing sectors are quite capital intensive, yet all the profits are achieved by the Sales operation. The Service segment, also a heavy user of capital, achieves completion for the sales transactions in the fields of operational assistance, repairs, parts, etc. Product profile or design, marketing, and advertising functions, may be set individually, at every level, according to the management's (Board of Directors) decisions.

A company can be engaged in all four segments, or only in one or two depending upon profile. As an example, a bank or any type of financial institution may have an R & D department, that researches and selects investment instruments, a department that "manufactures" those instruments, a department that sells them to the public, and a service group which takes care of various aspects related to the administration of those new financial instruments, such as posting interest, redemptions, etc.

An auto maker would have this structure of economic activity much more visible through the public exposure that goes with all the efforts to entice the customer to buy a specific auto product.

Karl Marx never worked one day in his life, never invested anything, so he was totally oblivious to the simple economic realities of the day. He delighted in creating the impression that most economic activities are a battle field between labor and capital. The notion of a free exchange of values between the participants in economic activities never entered his mind. He proposed a type of socialism where the "proletarians" take everything the upper classes have, but never asked the question of what happens after the proletarians run out of the other people's money. The collapse of most all communist regimes was caused by the perversion of the economic model to a two dimensional diagram with the government on one side, and the masses on the other. There was no profit motivation and the economy was stagnant. No one gives 100% freely or enthusiastically for the benefit of an abstract ideology!

In spite of the disastrous failures of all Marxist-Leninist regimes there are lots of economists who propose the same economic model, for the US, especially in the academia. Redistributing income, from producers, to the loafers, has always been a favorite with Marxists.

If the government becomes a major partner, or the owner, of every type of economic activity, as the Marxist-Leninists propose, the profit motive is dead, and the entire thing reverts to what Lech Walesa defined so eloquently in 1980, about the essence of the Polish socialist system:

"They fake that they pay us, we fake that we work."

From this short discussion it should be evident that the Marxist theory of "non-market" economy is a superstition, at best, or a malicious subversion to rob the masses they profess to "love", of basic economic human dignity.

When such ideas permeate our governments and the leftist media sings a lot of odes to such concepts, hide your checkbook, and head for the polls, to oust all the rascals.

There is no other scientific superstition, responsible for more human suffering and death, that this idea of universal equity through socialism.

8. The Population Explosion
A scientific superstition for readucing the globe's population through genocide

The idea that our planet is stressed to the maximum, by too many people populating it, is another superstition sustained by some segments of the scientific community. That is nothing new. Ancient philosophers, like Plato, (423-347 BC) and Cicero, (106-43 BC) raised serious questions in connection with an apparent issue of overpopulation.

In 405 BC, Plato stated that:

"If we cannot stop the influx of people moving to our city, we will be all chocked by masses who will endanger our wealth."

For a relatively small Greek city-state, the crowding of people inside the walled and fortified community, created a lot of problems from health to crime. That's why the ancient Greeks restricted who could reside in a city.

Cicero, familiar with the works of Plato and other Greek philosophers, lamented in 79 BC:

"There is no reason for anyone to bring his slaves to the city. There are, already, too many people here. The place of a slave is in the fields to tend to the crops and to the livestock."

Cicero lived in Rome, during a period of civil unrest and wars, when every general or person of means maintained households with hundreds of soldiers, servants and slaves. In order to minimize the effects of crowding in the Rome, Caius Julius Caesar, just before his death, instituted one-way streets in the city, in order to facilitate rapid passage for chariots, in 44 BC.

In modern times, as an extension of Darwinism, several thinkers came with the idea that too many people on the planet ruin the quality of life for all.

Thomas Robert Malthus, (1766-1843) studied the economic model of the day and created mathematical representations of most of relationships between population size and resources, establishing that:

"The increase in population is limited by the means of subsistence, and the population increases when the means of subsistence increase."

Such an observation seemed logical for a colonial empire at the turn of the 19th century. Malthus furthermore, postulated that the population grows at a geometric ratio, while the resources can only be developed in a simple, arithmetic ratio.

In his book, "An Essay on the Principle of Population", published in 1798, Malthus argues that the population growth follows times of plenty, in terms of food and commodities, until a saturation point is reached. When that happens, the society, as a whole, experiences economic distress, with the lower classes being affected the most.

Malthus recognizes the "beneficial" effects of epidemics, droughts and wars, as "natural" regulators of the population growth:

"The vices of mankind are active and able ministers of depopulation, capable to bring order to chaos."

In an objective retrospect, one has to give Malthus credit for the validity of his reasoning, especially when you realize that he could not benefit of valid, ample statistical data at that time. Nevertheless, his theory is still the darling of many academics and scientific researchers, including some in the UN employment.

The population of the entire world, in his days, was probably around one billion people. Contrast that with the 7.025 billion we had in 2013. The nature of the human being changed very little, over the years, even if our society became a Type II civilization, capable to leave the planet. The basic factors affecting population levels are still the same: a function of resources versus expectations.

The population density in the world averages 39.7 people per square km. (Asia 86.7, Africa 32.8, Europe 70.0, North America 23.0, South America 22.0, and Oceania 4.25 per UN population data). The population of London, in 1800, was over 88 people per square km, comparable to that found today in Asia.

The Earth's surface consists of approximately 360 million square km of water, and slightly over 150 million square km of land, out of which only some 100 million square km are inhabitable and fit for agriculture.

To insure proper food production, there should be a minimum of 5 acres of worked, arable land, for every person. By properly interpolating all the data concerning population and arable land, it would be evident that the planet could support a population double its current size. If you factor in the hydrosphere (oceans, rivers and lakes) you would see that the additional sources of food represented by fish and aquatic organisms can go a long way to provide sustenance for all mankind, at much higher population levels.

Then, what is the cause for alarm? Why does the UN advocate a reduction in population, by 50%, before the end of the 21st century, through its Agenda 21 summits?

Let's examine, for a moment, the population distribution. During the last century, the attraction of large, industrial cities, proved irresistible for large segments of rural dwellers. That caused a massive dislocation of those people, from agriculture, to urban areas, on every single continent. The allure of wages and public support, proved much stronger than the traditions of land cultivation. That phenomenon increased the "misery index" in most every country, cementing the demarcation line between poor and rich folks. And that is the single most important aspect that motivates the advocates of drastic measures of world population reduction.

As a mathematical model, some researchers created two exercises, in which the entire world population was "transferred" to France, first, and then to Canada. The results were shocking, but similar.

By placing all the world population (7.025 billion people) in France, (area of 675,000 square km, or 265,000 square miles) the population density would be around 105 people per square km, less than that of Tokyo, Mumbai or Singapore. The agricultural basis, however, would not be able to support such a population concentration.

In the second example, the entire world population was "placed" in Canada, which has an area of 10 million square km or 3.9 million square miles. The population density would reach some 70 people per square km, or 28 people per square mile. (All this data comes from the North American Econometric Institute, a think tank for futurists.)

As a sterile mathematical speculation these examples do not prove much, except for the fact that physically the Earth could hold just about double the number of current inhabitants with no significant change in the current standard of living..

What these models also prove, is that, if all the planet's population is being concentrated in relatively small areas, with not a single soul in the rest of the world, survival would be possible. Quality of life, however, is a totally different thing. Defenders of this point of view argue that the rest of the world's lands and waters could provide enough resources to insure the harmonious development within a society well-balanced along the line of production-consumption axis.

Is then, the man his own worst enemy? Hardly. It would take a great deal of ignorance and arrogance, to dare to advance this type of thinking. It is true that the "poverty index" is highest in the most populous countries, but the real cause is not the population structure but the economic system used. All the countries with a high standard of living have free market economies, while the poorest countries in the world, are chocked by byzantine rules set by dictators and war lords, under the name of absolute political control.

Our planet does not suffer from overpopulation, but from a lack of planning and misguided political forces which promote unnatural ideas and ideologies that dehumanize in mass.

Standardizing the lowest common denominator as a "scientific approach" to world population management is a cruel superstition. Which ethnic group, shall be exterminated first?

Anthropologists and economists point to the extremely important relation between population composition and food production patterns. Any large population concentration necessitates "green belts" around them, in order to insure the production of agricultural commodities. That includes the vegetables, meat, fish, cereals and dairy products. And that is the secret of an acceptable living standard.

If you survey the economic positioning of the largest metropolitan areas, you will find that readily available food supply reinforce Malthus' findings. Mexico City, Cairo, Tokyo, Moscow, and New York, all are some of the most congested areas in the world, yet their populations have a solid agricultural support basis. Within 25 miles from any of those cities there are a lot of agricultural production belts. Factoring access to rapid transportation and means of distribution, such cities can guaranty a relatively good level of general consumption. And that is the basis for maintaining an acceptable index of life satisfaction, in spite of what the prophets of gloom and doom predict for the next two centuries.

An accurate assessment of the population picture shall incorporate all the elements related to mortality and births. The trend is definitely much more conducive to increases in population, due primarily to more efficient health care and better nutrition, while the birth rates are dropping in most all industrialized nations. That seems unable to sustain the minimum birth rate of 2.1per couple, in order to maintain a stable level. A contributing factor to population shift in composition, is caused by various local customs, such as polygamy and certain religious tenets primarily based on superstitions.

Regions of the world, with concentrated masses of Muslims, will cause an offset in population distribution, regardless the regional availability of resources. That will determine a continuation of famine, epidemics and regional wars. The population explosion is silent, it never created a bang.

9. Diseases and Vaccines
Not all vaccines are safe when states regulate everything

Most everybody knows what a vaccine is, but very few people know that the word is derived from the Latin "vacca", meaning "cow". It was the fluid from a diseased cow, infected with cow pox that was "injected" into a human to alleviate or prevent the symptoms of chicken pox. That technique was first introduced in the early 1700s.

The vaccination consists in the introduction of a pathogen into a body, in order to create an acquired immunity to a certain disease. It is equivalent to a hard protein shock to the autoimmune system, which usually stimulates the creation of specialized antibodies to fight the microscopic invaders.

Generally the public uses the terms "vaccination" and "inoculation" interchangeably even though there is a marked difference between the two methods of creating immunity to pathogens. Dr. Louis Pasteur (1822-1895), described best the differences:

"Vaccination actually consists of injecting deactivated toxins or some with reduced potency, taken from a cow infected with cow pox. The process of inoculation is a bit more complex, and has been practiced for ages: as an example, the live smallpox virus is taken from a pustule or a scab from an infected patient and it is injected under the skin of the person desiring to gain immunity to this disease."

By the year 1450 the European doctors made a distinction between the **smallpox**, (variola) and the **great pox**, (syphilis) intuitively devising ways to prevent the spread of smallpox trough quite primitive inoculation methods. (The smallpox ravaged native American populations after the first contacts with the Europeans.)

There is no controversy surrounding the medical benefits of most vaccines, however, during the second part of the 20th century, various voices, some more qualified than others, raised surprising issues, such as the high occurrence of pediatric cancers in children vaccinated at an early age, and a some of the psychiatric illnesses were connected to inoculations, as was the attention deficit disorder, (ADD), in preteens.

Some statistical data underlined the apparent connections along the lines just mentioned above. That determined the scientific community to reexamine the vaccines used and to follow many subjects through life-long studies, way beyond childhood.

The first method of vaccine production is that of inactivated toxins, and it was recently re-examined in detail. The virus or bacteria responsible for the disease is, most of the time, grown in lab cultures and then killed with either heat, microwaves of formaldehyde. If properly processed, this vaccine is safe, since only the outer protein of the microorganism survives. The immune system will recognize this protein and the microphages will eliminate it when the real McCoy enters the organism. The virus or the bacteria is dead and cannot multiply, yet some unforeseen problems have been discovered infrequently.

Formaldehyde molecules attach to the vaccine protein creating an abnormal cellular development in the receiving patient's tissues. That is cancer. Through the "deactivation process" the protein intended to "train" the immune system becomes subject to various unexpected macro-molecular changes. The microwave bombardment, during the "deactivation process", may render the entire process useless. Pharmaceutical companies, all over the world, were forced to adjust and retool this process, fact which caused serious shortages of vaccines on all continents, prompting over-regulation..

The second method of vaccine production, that which creates a type known as "attenuated toxin vaccine", uses live microorganisms, stressed by radiation and strong electro-magnetic fields, so that they lose the ability to reproduce, thus making an easy target for the macrophage cells. Due to some improper manufacturing processes, mass-vaccinations in Asia and Africa caused massive outbreaks of infectious diseases. The pharmaceutical companies involved denied any responsibility, and quit producing several types of vaccines.

The "particulate protein vaccine", considered a break-through in the pharmaceutical technology, is basically a designer protein, which resembles the molecular structure of the protein of the offending virus. The unintended consequence of this production process was found to consist in the ability of these proteins to combine into larger chains, which the immune system no longer will recognize. Some of the resulting "combined proteins" will affect the patient's DNA, eliminating a lot of the components of the auto-immune system.

Researchers and scientists, on all continents, vehemently deny any reason for alarm in connection with the safety of vaccine production, citing the low statistical prevalence of this type of problems. But that, in itself, is another scientific superstition.

Many other methods of producing vaccines, most notably in UK, USA, Canada and China, start from the premise that if the immune system can be determined to produce defensive reactions to microorganisms, then any molecule resembling that pathogen will do the job. To some extent that is true. The problems arise when the designer aims for one thing and the living matter which is the toxic protein, starts to take unexpected directions. When introduced into a human body, these proteins may cause the immune system to work "overtime" under severe forms of allergic reactions. That will happen also with "natural" proteins treated with radiation.

Dr. Horea Porumb, a French biophysicist, in an interview with the Swiss television, stated in 2012, that the radiation technology used in the pharmaceutical industry:

"..it is quite safe for producing important vaccines, yet, the DNA chains of the original microorganisms can be modified in unexpected ways, fact which requires additional research."

This has been one of the first cases when a scientist of world-class stature recognized that there is a lot of scientific superstition attached to the style and structure of designer proteins used as vaccines.

From here to the next step taken by the US government scientists is a lot of distance. I am referring to the efforts to mass vaccinate large urban centers in America and Canada, by the use of mild pathogens dispersed from the air, over the largest cities. This action came to fruition after the 911 events, and focused on air-spraying vaccines for anthrax, typhoid fever and several other highly infectious diseases, as in the case of an bacteriological doomsday scenario. The areas covered include New York, Chicago, Los Angeles, San Francisco, Dallas, Miami, Saint Paul, Houston, Seattle and Washington, DC. Anyone can imagine the huge costs involved, yet the practical justification for such an action is extremely hard to ascertain.

The main beneficiaries were the pharmaceutical companies that a skeptic would connect to specific electoral contributions,

In 1998, a research paper, published by the Englishman Dr. Andrew Wakefield, in The Lancet, pointed to an apparent connection between the MMR Vaccine, (for measles, mumps and rubella), and the onset of autistic symptoms in children.

The author of that paper was forced to retract his "suppositions", even though his statistical data was available for scrutiny. The Lancet retracted its editorial point of view, issuing a "mea culpa" for publishing the material. The pressure from the pharmaceutical companies was too great to bear. All the work Dr. Wakefield did in the field of vaccine research was labeled as "irrelevant", thus invalid

As a consumer of medical services, the average person is totally oblivious to what's going on behind the doors of secretive labs. If those people who create new medicines and new medical technologies say that they work well, who are we to doubt that?

In fact that's how scientific superstitions survive for long time.

Michael Brooks, in his book "Free Radicals", (2012), describes the general atmosphere in the pharmaceutical research and in and around the scientific community, as "anarchy", placing the blame on research sponsors and regulators. He makes a valid case against "scientists behaving badly".

And that's the point where scientific superstitions get institutionalized.

The food and drug regulators, specifically the US Food and Drug Administration (FDA), are extremely slow and, most of the time will only react to what the market does. Obviously the main preoccupation is not with the safety of food or drug production, but with the Big-Brother control. If there is no reason for regulators to get involved, they will find a way to stick their hand in all pockets. They place an inordinately excessive attention on the consumption of raw milk, which is a cultural tradition with many groups, such as the Mexican Americans, the Amish and the Black farmers, trying to eliminate practices not condoned by the giant of the dairy industry.

Our vast government bureaucracy already tells us what kind of food or drugs we may ingest, how we are allowed to educate our children, and what we can and cannot say to each other. "Political Correctness", reasons. (PC) have to prevail at all costs. Our Big-Brother Government is the largest purveyor of crass scientific superstitions.

But that aspect is not limited to the federal structure. The extent of states following federal lack of common sense, was recently illustrated, in 2011, by the Texas Commission on Environmental Quality, (TCEQ), which Investigated a complaint, and set in motion a lot of controversy, spending an inordinate amount of time, money and energy on a trivial issue.

The complaint was about the hunters in the Limestone County, in Texas, who were defecating in the woods. The TCEQ wrote a letter to the county judge, Daniel Burkeen, instructing him to intervene to "correct" this problem, with potentially grave health issues..

After the judge researched the state's statutes and regulations, he found that the TCEQ strictly prohibited outhouses in the Texas public wild areas. (Is this a free country, or what?)

In another brilliant example of lack of bureaucratic synchronization of rules and regulations, the Occupational Safety and Health Administration, (OSHA), requires that all the work places where animals are slaughtered or processed , have to have perfectly dry floors, in order to prevent slippage. The FDA, on the other hand, requires that the same work places need to have the floors hosed down, every four hours with bacteriostatic and germicidal agents, to prevent bacterial growth.

In another arrogant stance, FDA devotes vast resources to prevent the American consumers from having access to raw milk:

"There is no 'deeply rooted' tradition of unfettered access to foods of all kinds." (Farm-to-Consumer Legal Defense Fund v. FDA, Iowa D.C., 2011)

The same agency, charged with the testing and evaluation of all new pharmaceuticals, takes, on the average, over ten years to allocate any of the necessary resources to approve the new products. In many cases that kind of work is of such an inferior quality, that frequently, after one or two years of marketing, the products are banned altogether due to too many fatal cases.

Unfortunately, our oversized government is here to stay, while its solid drive for the creation of the most blatant scientific superstitions in the field of vaccines or related health disciplines will only get stronger.

The benefits to the vast majority of consumers are never a concern.

Everything is done in the name of the process.

Scientific superstitions have impressive longevity!

"A government big enough to give you everything you want, is big enough to take away everything you have." (Thomas Jefferson)

What you need to retain from this short discussion on vaccines, is the fact that any idea, no matter how brilliant, can be perverted to something useless or dangerous, simply by ignoring common sense in applying it.

Then what is a scientific superstition? It is a malicious half-truth, used specifically to enhance a scientific process, or to torpedo it.

The regulators, based on scientific superstitions, went as far as to declare prohibitions against the proliferation of entire lists of species of plants and animals, even if most of them lived on this Earth considerably longer than the humans.

If you think that the Drug Enforcement Administration, (DEA), or the Food and Drug Administration, (FDA), are going to stop decreeing what you can legally eat, inhale or drink, think again. After all the American milk production will be forced to be tied to the new FDA specification, the list of possible candidates will include, most likely, eggs, poultry, venison, fish and wines.

Isn't that a pretty picture?

Along the same nebulous thinking process, the Environmental Protection Agency, (EPA), is requiring farmers to file costly emergency management plans for dealing with the possible "disasters" of spilled milk, to show how they'd train first responders and how they'd build containment facilities for such accidents. EPA, normally, oversees the cleanup of oil spills. Someone may assume that because milk contains some fat or oily molecules, the dangers of spills may be just as damaging to the environment as the crude oil spills.

The farmers will have to spend time and money to compile all the required documentation. The additional costs will be passed on to the food consumers, together with the bill for countless new EPA employees hired to administer the program, to inspect farms, to detect and punish any of the non-compliant red-necks . That's not an elegant way to create jobs!

Before the scientific superstitions became institutionalized, at the national level, they were limited only to a small circle of specialists. Not anymore.

An international consortium of pharmaceutical companies, under a contract with the UN's International Health Organization, synchronizes the manufacture of some 20 million doses of mumps vaccine for several African countries. The manufacturer shipped the initial volume of doses and billed the sponsor for double of the amount shipped. It is estimated that the extra billing was necessary to cover the bribes imposed by local governments and their officials, a fact quite customary there. After serious medical scrutiny it was found that most of the mumps vaccine units were ineffective.

The manufacturer blamed either the lack of refrigeration, or the excessive refrigeration for the snafu.

An outbreak of mumps in Central Africa, in 2005, forced the UN's IHO to require the replacement of the entire stock of vaccine.

Some British journalists commented sarcastically, that because the mumps affect male fertility, the UN should have continued to use ineffective vaccines, if not for nothing else, for population control.

A short analysis of the institutional traditions in the manufacture of vaccines, can allow a reader to form an educated opinion about the main types of thinking on a collision course between medical science and all the "scientific superstitions" generated in the process of chasing the dollar.

43

10. Homosexuality
Genetic mental disease, or learned behavior?

The homosexual behavior is an aberrant human relation known from antiquity. It encompasses several groups: gays, (men who prefer to practice anal intercourse with another man), lesbians, (women who derive sexual satisfaction through mutual masturbation), bisexuals, (people who like to have sexual intercourse with men and women), and transvestites,(people who act as they were of opposite sex)

In antiquity homosexual practices were considered proof of virility, when a man overcame another man through brute physical force, and as an act of adding insult to injury, raped the victim. The Greek and Roman art and literature are full of examples of "homosexual love".

The lesbians are considered to have originated on the North-Aegean Greek island of Lesbos (or Lesvos), where after a series of wars the free men were banned from the island. The population of noble women delighted in music and poetry, worshiped local gods in elaborate temples and they only maintained sexual relations with each other. All the work was performed by castrate male slaves who had no right to enter the cities. The legend has it that due to very low birth rates the population dwindled down to extinction being easily taken over by "barbarians" such as the Hittite and the Persians.

Associating today's lesbians with the classical Greek model, is an immature attempt to convey the resemblance of "class" to an abject sexual practice.

Bisexuals and transvestites are the product of modern decadence and have no historical models to claim.

Most all religions condemn homosexual behavior as an unnatural activity, contrary to God's laws

Judeo-Christian, Muslim, Buddhist and Native American religions and believes, all ostracize homosexuals.

The Koran, through the Sharia laws, and several hadiths (religious decrees), mention the "liwat", (homosexual intercourse) as an unpardonable sin against Allah:

"When a man mounts another, the throne of god shakes...", and "Kill the one that is doing it, and the one that is being done to."

(Koran 7:80)

This sin is connected to the biblical Hebrew story of Sodom and Gomorrah, with entire complements of fire and brimstone, (Koran 7-64)

Interestingly enough, the Ottoman (Turks) clerics decreed in early 1300s, that the Koran only prohibits sex acts with men, never mentioning any young boys, thus sex acts with boys were permitted. That's why this kind of promiscuity was rampant in the Ottoman Empire.

The recent drive, in some of the developed nations, to recognize the homosexuals as a minority with special rights along the lines of sexual preferences, is intensifying at every level, as an anti-religious movement. That wouldn't create much of a controversy, however, without the effort of an "educational process" of converting youngsters to an "alternate style of life". That is the straw that breaks the camel's back.

The same sex marriages, pushed by extreme leftists, flies in the face of American traditions and values. To see Rohm Emmanuel, the mayor of Chicago, a Jew, holding hands with Louis Farrakhan, a vowed anti-Semitic leader of the Nation of Islam, in blasting the Chick-fill-a management, for not endorsing the same sex marriage idea, is, at least strange.

Homosexuality contributes directly to the disintegration of the US family as a viable social institution, creating whole generations of welfare clients and jail inmates. The facts are irrefutable, yet several "scientists" find ways to legitimize homosexuality as a biological necessity for specific sets of DNA characteristics, divorcing the act from any moral connotations and justifying everything through physiology and psychology.

That's how one of the most repulsive scientific superstitions was created toward the end of the 20th century. The Hollywood and the main "progressive" media, jumped on this idea, pushing for special laws to grant the homosexuals some rights that the heterosexuals never had, through the concepts of hate-speech and hate-crime.

Judeo-Christian religious practices have been attacked constantly for "discriminating" against homosexuals by defining their practices as sins.

The first ever study of human homosexual practices, in 1948, by Dr. Alfred Kinsey, was synthesized in his study, "Sexual Behavior in the Human Male" and created a storm of controversy polarizing the scientific community, either for, or against his conclusions.

He devised the so-called "Kinsey Scale", which evaluates all the possible types of sexual activity from "0", (no homosexual experiences), to "6", (exclusively homosexual experiences). Later an "X" grade was used for asexuality. Some years later the study was extended to women subjects.

What the Kinsey research did, was to find a common cause-effect relationship between social elements and environmental factors, just as Dr.

Sigmund Freud (1856-1939) did earlier.

While this, and subsequent studies, started from the premise that homosexuality, under all its forms of manifestation, is an aberrant, unnatural or a dysfunctional activity, it was assumed that, as a normal variation in the human sexuality, it does not cause negative psychological effects. Later on, based on extensive research by the team of William Masters, PhD, and Virginia Johnson, PhD, it was concluded that, due to certain social and religious norms, homosexual activities stress the participants through segregation and marginalization, to the point of psychological trauma.

The "sexual revolution" of the 1960s and 1970s, enrolled notable modern researchers in the field of physiology and genetics, to prove and cement the idea that homosexuality is a matter of "genetic predisposition", codified in the DNA structure of certain individuals with affinity for it. This approach, considered "elegant", separated completely the notion of sexual orientation from any norms of moral or rational considerations.

And this is the way another scientific superstition was born.

Of course, the homosexual activists, all over the world, jumped on this platform of scientific "proofs" to further their causes.

In 1983, the Brazilian gay magazine, "Cabinhero", meaning "Cabin Boy", published several articles to "prove" that most of the world's geniuses were gay. On that occasion they commemorated 100 years from the death of Karl Marx, (1818-1883), the founder of "scientific socialism". In a series of articles they paid tribute to Marx's homosexual relation with his mentor, Friedrich Engels, (1820-1895), describing in detail the fights between Marx and his rabbi of the synagogue he frequented. After several confrontations, in which the rabbi stressed the sinful nature of homosexuality, as a violation of God's Law, Karl Marx abandoned his Jewish roots and was baptized a Lutheran. The Brazilian magazine considered this an act of exemplary courage, citing the fact that Karl Marx and Friedrich Engels were much more influential, in the history of humanity, than Jesus Christ and all the world's philosophers put together. (If you think of it, they may be right. No other ideology killed over 200 million innocent people, in less than one century!)

In 1886, the German doctor Richard Von Krafft-Ebing published a book titled "Psychopathia Sexualis" , (Sexual Psychopathy) in which he described over 200 sexual acts he considered abnormal, or pathological, stating that the human sexual orientation is a matter of learned behavior and it is not an instinctive reflex based on genetics.

That point of view was not challenged until in the 1950s, when the American Association of Practicing Psychiatrists published its annual report, in 1952, in the Manual of Mental Health, Diagnostic, Treatment and Statistics. It classified all homosexual manifestations as mental diseases.

Under considerable pressure from certain gay politicians, the medical classification of homosexuality was removed from the list of mental ills, in 1975.

The UN's World Health Organization, in its ICD-10 document for the year 1997, listed homosexuality as a severe mental illness. Most of the world's health specialists representing UN members voted unanimously to adopt this document's findings and language.

American media representatives, especially around Hollywood, did protest the UN classification, calling for a boycott of UNESCO and many other UN groups, pressuring the US to abstain from financing the UNESCO.

In 1985, the California-based "Gay and Lesbian Education Fund", obtained a significant grant from the United Way, and underwrote a massive research effort to prove, once for all, that homosexuality has a genetic basis. They hired some of the best geneticists, bio-physicist and clinicians, who went to work on this "Rainbow Project".

After over ten years of research, the project's lead geneticist, Dr. Aaron Cohen wrote in the final paper that:

"... according to extensive research work, on more than 2,000 DNA samples from gay men and lesbian women, no one was able to isolate a gene responsible for homosexual behavior. That is an activity one learns from his or her peers."

Dr. Aaron Cohen was summarily dismissed by that project's sponsor, illustrating, once more, that true scientific work cannot coexist with biased, predetermined objectives. That's how the official birth certificate of another scientific superstition was rubber-stamped, sealed and delivered.

Currently there is no consensus among scientists about any genetic or physiological factors which may determine a person's sexual orientation.

In a paper issued in 2007, the UK's College of Psychiatrists stated unequivocally, that:

"Despite almost one century of studies and thousands of volumes of psychoanalytical and physiological speculations, there is not a single bit of substantive evidence to support the suggestion of a natural or genetic connection with any homosexual activity."

In an article published in the American Pediatric Review, in 2009,

47

Dr. A. Collins, discussing child sexuality and homosexual tendencies, states that:

"Homosexuality is a choice established in early childhood. The young boys and girls are more likely to experiment with friends of same sex."

The author also noted that the age of sexual awareness among children gets younger and younger. He observed also, that homosexual child prostitution is an alarming phenomenon that has to be stopped, if the human race is to survive, in view of declining birth rates. His observations caused a barrage of insults and threats from consecrated gay and lesbian activists.

In an article in the online publication LGBTLife.com (LGBT stands for Lesbian, Gay, Bisexual and Transvestites), one of the contributors stated, in 2010, that :

"Most gay and lesbian acts with children are beneficial for their full and harmonious development."

Such statements and the drive to bring more children "to appreciate the alternate life styles", are absolutely unacceptable, no matter who you are.

The press reports during the last few decades are full of examples where people in charge of youngsters abused them sexually. That included figures of authority, such as priests, preachers, judges, coaches, etc.

In an elaborate study finished in 2008, its author, Dr. D. F. Swab. reintroduced in discussion the genetic aspect of homosexual behavior as having a congenital dimension:

"The fetal brain develops during its intra-uterine stage, in a distinct male direction, due to the effects of testosterone on the nervous system, or in a female direction, under the effects of testosterone absence, regardless, its neurological or somatic developmental form. This is irrefutable proof that the homosexual orientations are determined genetically, long before the birth, by factors not yet fully understood."

Does anybody think that there could be a more illustrative example of a scientific superstition?

Vociferous homosexual activists use such "scientific" research to determine the American politicians to include the sexual orientation in the list of constitutionally-protected categories, on par with race, nationality, sex religion, and age.

From here, to the point where same sex marriage is ubiquitous, the same gay and lesbian activists hope to be just a small step, yet, all over the country, this idea was rejected at the ballot box. The marriage, between a man and a woman has been the basic social institution ever since the humans exited the ancestral cave, and there is no reason to change that now, even if we just became a Type II civilization, capable to leave the planet.

Public acceptance of homosexual behavior is lowest in Africa, Asia, and Australia, highest in Europe and America.

As one Dutch prime minister recently expressed his country's point of view on this subject, other nations implement similar policies:

"It is nobody's business what two consenting adults do in private, but as soon as they involve immature children, the state has to put a stop to it."

Sometimes the line between science and superstition, is very finely defined, and many human passions can modify a valid point of view.

The merit of any position in the contest between ideas dealing with the homosexuality, is relative, and its degree of acceptance or rejection ,by the general public, reflects the aura of traditional values of the society.

There is nothing objective in the position of most gay activists who fight for "recognition" as valid social groups, or an alternate cultural current.

At this point, some sarcastic journalists, quoting the fact that some Roman emperor married his horse, ask that if the same-sex marriages will be recognized, when will it be legal to marry your pet. (The tax angles for such additional dependent deductions, if so legislated, could be of an immense advantage.)

There is absolutely no reason to bring to the front of popular culture and conscience, any of the aberrant sexual displays the minority of the gay community wants to impose upon the majority of people.

Even though antagonistic, the notions of "gay' and "straight" people can coexist peacefully, as long as the gays use their own closets and do not force the entire society to foot the bill for their characteristic ills. On another note, the objection to the actions of popularized homosexual behavior in the media, shall be restricted above the level of legal consent.

It is the consensus of most researchers that protecting the children, from predatory homosexuals and pedophiles, is an intrinsic governmental function, that shall not be delegated to the gay community.

No matter what you think about homosexuals, whether the affliction they suffer from is pathological or not, just about all sexual activities are definitely learned, including sadism, bestiality and other sex crimes.

49

11. Epilogue

How do you avoid being victimized by the academia

An epilogue is placed at the end of a piece of work to serve as a closing statement regarding the main ideas expressed by the author. It is not a mandatory part of every book, but, if used, can add a dimension of thought provoking review.

The main points I would like you to remember are:

The scientific work requires an extensive preparation in terms of education and expenditures;

The scientists never start their work based on the idea to convince the public of falsehoods;

The perversion of bona-fide research work occurs in the context of sponsor-selected goals and objectives;

Some scientists prostitute themselves intellectually, in order to continue receiving a salary;

The half-truths, the false relations, and the baseless assumptions that are passed on as "scientific facts", give birth to scientific superstitions;

The ignorant members of the media popularize those superstitions, ad nauseam, getting the general public to accept and to believe in them;

Ignorance and a decaying educational system are the best allies to insure longevity for scientific superstitions;

When the scientific superstitions become institutionalized by being adopted at any level, be it local, state, national or international, the society may be in for shockingly painful disasters, socially economically, and, of course, politically;

There is no effective defense against scientific superstitions, outside the process of educating you and your family, in basic scientific theories, which one would expect to learn in high school.

BIBLIOGRAPHY

- IPCC AR4 WG1 (2007). "Summary for Policymakers". In Solomon, S.; Qin, D.; Manning, M.; Chen, Z.; Marquis, M.; Averyt, K.B.; Tignor, M.; and Miller, H.L. *Climate Change 2007: The Physical Science Basis*. Contribution of Working Group I to the Fourth Assessment Report of the Intergovernmental Panel on Climate Change. Cambridge University Press. ISBN 978-0-521-88009-1 (pb: 978-0-521-70596-7).
- IPCC AR4 SYR (2007). "Summary for Policymakers". In Core Writing Team; Pachauri, R.K; and Reisinger, A. *Climate Change 2007: Synthesis Report*. Contribution of Working Groups I, II and III to the Fourth Assessment Report of the Intergovernmental Panel on Climate Change. IPCC. ISBN 92-9169-122-4.
- Emanuel K (August 2005). "Increasing destructiveness of tropical cyclones over the past 30 years" (PDF). *Nature* **436** (7051): 686–8. Bibcode:2005Natur.436..686E. doi:10.1038/nature03906. PMID 16056221.
- Edwards, Paul Geoffrey; Miller, Clark A. (2001). *Changing the atmosphere: expert knowledge and environmental governance*. Cambridge, Mass: MIT Press. ISBN 0-262-63219-5.
- McKibben, Bill (2011). The Global Warming Reader. New York, N.Y.: OR Books. ISBN 978-1-935928-3• Common Misconceptions about Icebergs and Glaciers". Ohio State University. "Icebergs float in salt water, but they are formed from freshwater glacial ice."

"Iceberg". *Online Etymology Dictionary*. Retrieved 2006-03-26.
- ^ Jump up to: *a* *b* "Facts on Icebergs". *Canadian Geographic*. Retrieved 2010-12-08.
"Antarctica shed a 208-mile-long berg in 1956". *Polar Times* 43. 2005-01-20. p. 18.
"Iceberg A-38B off South Georgia". *Visible Earth*. Retrieved 2011-03-09.
"Huge ice sheet breaks from Greenland glacier". BBC. 2010-08-07. Retrieved 2011-03-
"Massive Iceberg Crashes Into Island• Stefan Riedel, MD, PhD (January 2005).
"Edward Jenner and the history of smallpox and vaccination". *Proceedings (Bayl Univ Med Cent)* **18** (1): 21–25. PMC 1200696.
Grammatikos, Alexandros P.; Mantadakis, Elpis; Falagas, Matthew E. (June 2009).
"Meta-analyses on Pediatric Infections and Vaccines". *Infectious Disease Clinics of North America* **23** (2): 431–57. doi:10.1016/j.idc.2009.01.008. PMID 19393917.
Neighmond, Patti (2010-02-07). "Adapting Vaccines For Our Aging Immune Systems". *Morning Edition* (NPR). Archived from the original on 2012-09-05. Retrieved 2014-01-09.
Sullivan, Patricia (2005-04-13). "Maurice R. Hilleman dies; created vaccines". *Wash. Post*. Archived from the original on 2012-09-15. Retrieved 2014-01-09.
Schlegel *et al.* (August 1999). "Comparative efficacy of three mumps vaccines during disease outbreak in eastern Switzerland: cohort study". *BMJ* **319** (7206): 352. doi:10.1136/bmj.319.7206.352. PMID 10435956. Retrieved 2014-01-09.
Préziosi, M.; Halloran, M.E. (2003). "Effects of Pertussis Vaccination on Disease: Vaccine Efficacy in Reducing Clinical Severity". *Clinical Infectious Diseases* (Oxford Journals) **37** (6): 772–779. doi:10.1086/377270.

Orenstein WA, Papania MJ, Wharton ME (2004). "Measles elimination in the United States". *J Infect Dis* **189** (Suppl 1): S1–3. doi:10.1086/377693. PMID 15106120.
• ^ Jump up to: *a* *b* *c* "Measles--United States, January 1-April 25, 2008". *Morb. Mortal. Wkly. Rep.* **57** (18): 494–8. May 2008. PMID 18463608.◌

"Vaccine Types". Niaid.nih.gov. 2012-04-03. Retrieved 2013-04-26.

J.K. Sinha & S. Bhattacharya. *A Text Book of Immunology* (Google Book Preview). Academic Publishers. p. 318. ISBN 978-81-89781-09-5. Retrieved 2014-01-09.

Kim W, Liau LM (2010). "Dendritic cell vaccines for brain tumors". *Neurosurg Clin N Am* **21** (1): 139–57. doi:10.1016/j.nec.2009.09.005. PMC 2810429. PMID 19944973.

Meri, S; Jördens, M; Jarva, H (December 2008). "Microbial complement inhibitors as vaccines". *Vaccine*. 26 Suppl 8: I113–7. doi:10.1016/j.vaccine.2008.11.058. PMID 19388175., Splits in Two".• Stefan Riedel, MD, PhD (January 2005). "Edward Jenner and the history of smallpox and vaccination". *Proceedings (Bayl Univ Med Cent)* **18** (1): 21–25. PMC 1200696.

Grammatikos, Alexandros P.; Mantadakis, Elpis; Falagas, Matthew E. (June 2009). "Meta-analyses on Pediatric Infections and Vaccines". *Infectious Disease Clinics of North America* **23** (2): 431–57. doi:10.1016/j.idc.2009.01.008. PMID 19393917.

Neighmond, Patti (2010-02-07). "Adapting Vaccines For Our Aging Immune Systems". *Morning Edition* (NPR). Archived from the original on 2012-09-05. Retrieved 2014-01-09.◌

Sullivan, Patricia (2005-04-13). *Wash. Post*. Archived from the original on 2012-09-15. Retrieved 2014-01-09.◌

Schlegel *et al.* (August 1999). "Comparative efficacy of three mumps vaccines during disease outbreak in eastern Switzerland: cohort study". *BMJ* **319** (7206): 352. doi:10.1136/bmj.319.7206.352. PMID 10435956. Retrieved 2014-01-09.◌

Préziosi, M.; Halloran, M.E. (2003). "Effects of Pertussis Vaccination on Disease: Vaccine Efficacy in Reducing Clinical Severity". *Clinical Infectious Diseases* (Oxford Journals) **37** (6): 772–779. doi:10.1086/377270.

Orenstein WA, Papania MJ, Wharton ME (2004). "Measles elimination in the United States". *J Infect Dis* **189** (Suppl 1): S1–3. doi:10.1086/377693. PMID 15106120.
b *c* "Measles--United States, January 1-April 25, 2008". *Morb. Mortal. Wkly. Rep.* **57** (18): 494–8. May 2008. PMID 18463608.◌

"Vaccine Types". Niaid.nih.gov. 2012-04-03. Retrieved 2013-04-26.

J.K. Sinha & S. Bhattacharya. *A Text Book of Immunology* (Google Book Preview). Academic Publishers. p. 318. ISBN 978-81-89781-09-5. Retrieved 2014-01-09.

Kim W, Liau LM (2010). "Dendritic cell vaccines for brain tumors". *Neurosurg Clin N Am* **21** (1): 139–57. doi:10.1016/j.nec.2009.09.005. PMC 2810429. PMID 19944973.

Meri, S; Jördens, M; Jarva, H (December 2008). "Microbial complement inhibitors as vaccines". *Vaccine*. 26 Suppl 8: I113–7. doi:10.1016/j.vaccine.2008.11.058. PMID 19388175.6-2

\

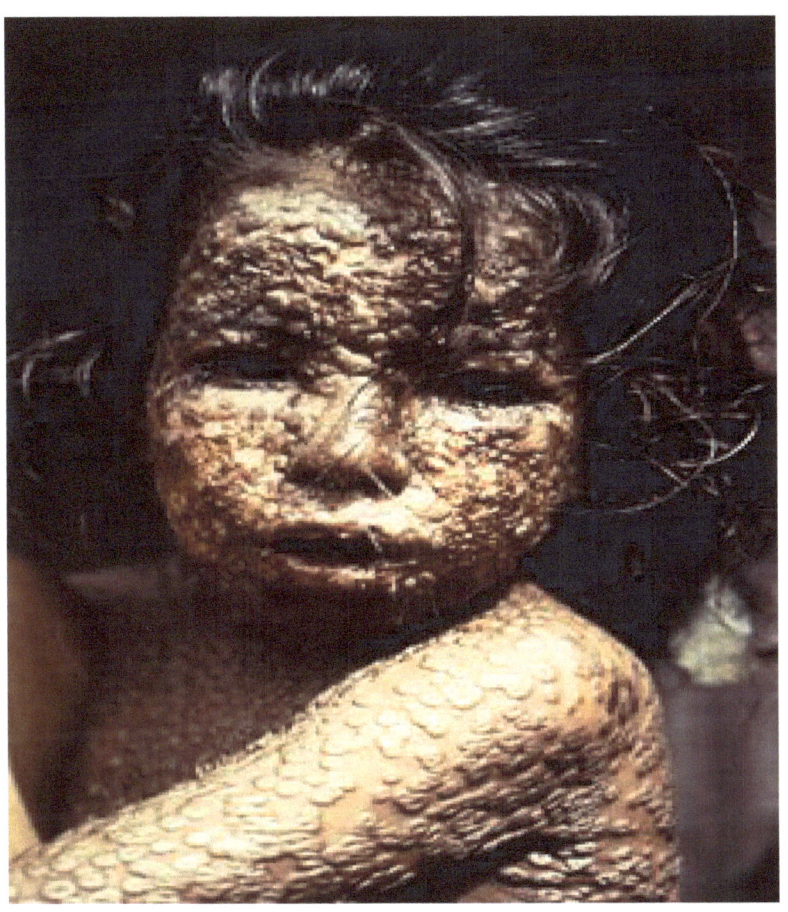

Child infected with smallpox in Nigeria, in 2012, in middle of an epidemic, which most health officials were convinced it couldn't ever happen, because of the quantity and quality of all vaccines administered by the International Health Organization to third world countries. (Photo courtesy Lillen AG)